Information Protection and Other Unnatural Acts

Information Protection and Other Unnatural Acts

Every Manager's Guide to Keeping Vital Computer Data Safe and Sound

Harry B. DeMaio

amacom
American Management Association

This publication is designed to provide accurate and authoritative
information in regard to the subject matter covered. It is sold with
the understanding that the publisher is not engaged in rendering
legal, accounting, or other professional service. If legal advice or
other expert assistance is required, the services of a competent
professional person should be sought.

Library of Congress Cataloging-in-Publication Data

DeMaio, Harry B.
    Information protection and other unnatural acts : every manager's
  guide to keeping vital computer data safe and sound / Harry B.
  DeMaio.
        p.   cm.
    Includes bibliographical references and index.
    ISBN 0-8144-5044-X (hard cover).—ISBN 0-8144-7780-1 (paperback)
    1. Computers—Access control. 2. Data protection. I. Title.
  QA76.9.A25D45   1991
  005.8—dc20   91-53053
                                                          CIP

Printing number

10   9   8   7   6   5   4   3   2   1

This book is
dedicated to
a very extraordinary bear.

Contents

Acknowledgments

While I take full responsibility for its content, it would be the height of arrogance and patently untrue for me to claim that every idea and concept contained in this book originated with me. On the other hand, it is also literally impossible to identify the origins of some of the material I've outlined.

The community of Information Protection specialists is rather small. Not only do most of us know each other, we rather freely exchange ideas and opinions with the usual balance of agreement and disagreement. So, the best I can do is list a number of individuals to whom I am certainly indebted for sharing their knowledge, opinions, and support.

At Deloitte & Touche, I want to offer sincere thanks to Everett Johnson, Bill Atkins, Toni Fish, Steve Ross, Cheryl Helsing, Doug Cale, Ann Finlayson, Myra Hess, Al Leech, Pamela Nelson, Gene Procknow, Tom Captain, Deborah Robinson, Frank Farrell, Bill Levant, Dave Lewis, Lee Curtis, Linda Stamm, Carl Jackson, Ron Hale, Mike Tyk, Chris Vandenoever, Kevin Stover, Joe O'Laughlin, Cy Devery, David Espitia, Maureen Vanacore, Dave Rosenstein, E. Terry Cowles, Trevor Gee, Gary Hardy, David Clark, Per Rhein Hansen, and Keiichi Kubo.

Among my other professional colleagues, I want to acknowledge the insights and invaluable opinions of Bill Murray, Carol Dye, Bob Courtney, Pamela Austin, Donn Parker, Hal Tipton, Curt Symes, Bill Whitehurst, Larry Wills, David Phelps, Mike Sobol, Fred Cohen, Martin Silverman, Jerry Lobel, Bob Jacobson, Jerry Fitzgerald, Lance Hoffman, Pat Gallagher, Sally Meglathery, John O'Leary, Rick Koenig, Roger Shaw, Bill Davis, John Geraghty, Ron Keelan, Sandra Lambert, Alan Krull, and many others.

There are a number of public institutions such as the National Institute of Justice, National Institute of Standards and Technology, and the National Computer Security Center, as well as many law enforcement agencies, that have contributed greatly to the state of computer security and my knowledge level.

In the private sector, I want to give special thanks to the IBM Corporation, Digital Equipment Co., Computer Associates, and a number of other companies that provide products that advance the security and continuity state of the art.

There are many organizations, such as the Information Systems Security Association, the Computer Security Institute, the EDP Auditors Association, the Institute of Internal Auditors, the International Institute for Information Integrity, and the International Information Systems Security Certification Consortium, Inc., who have provided me with major opportunities for the interchange of facts and ideas.

There are a number of publications and periodicals, many of which are mentioned in the bibliography in this book, to which I am sincerely indebted.

Finally, I am extremely grateful to the editorial staff at AMACOM Books for their patient handling and support of a fledgling author and most especially, to my wife, Virginia, and our two sons, Mark and Andrew, for their professional insights and loving encouragement.

Introduction

Protecting information is *not* natural. On the contrary, it runs counter to many of our deepest urges—intellectual curiosity, the need to communicate, the need to socialize, to trust and be trusted. In fact, we are usually suspicious of people or institutions that are secretive, regardless of their reasons. Nor are we consistent. While carefully trying to protect our own privacy, most of us are still fascinated by other people's scandals.

Humans and most animals have a strong protective sense when it comes to territory or tangible items—their assets. Try taking a bottle from a baby or a bone from a dog. Unfortunately, many information protection programs are based on the dangerous assumption that information is just another asset. If that were true, most people would protect information the same way they'd protect a wallet or a typewriter. They don't.

Information *is* different. Our attitudes and basic drives toward it are different. Any information protection program that assumes that good people will protect information simply by doing what comes naturally is doomed to failure. That's because seeking and sharing are our natural inclinations when it comes to information. That conflict of objectives is basic and needs to be clearly understood and addressed by managers planning an information protection program.

Before microprocessors and distributed systems came on the scene, resulting in computers appearing on virtually every desk top, this issue would have been interesting but academic. Today, it is of paramount importance, because the more we depend on sophisticated technology for processing information, the more we depend on people.

The Information Processing Environment

Market surveys, business and technical publications, managers, and specialists all agree: Information processing is changing and will continue to change dramatically throughout the 1990s.

The following have all made efficient, effective, and well-controlled information processing a critical success factor for most businesses, governments, and institutions:

- New hardware and software technologies
- High-capacity and cost-effective communications
- New applications
- Expanding user communities
- Increasing market demands

Without responsive and appropriate information processing capabilities, an organization may lose its competitive edge. Its reputation for quality and service, cost control, and profitability—perhaps even its continued existence—could be at stake. Even in enterprises in which security, continuity, and control of information resources have never been issues before, managers at all levels are beginning to realize that history may not be a reliable indicator of the future. Compromise or failure of information systems is becoming all too probable in today's highly interconnected world. The impact of such compromise or failure is also becoming more serious.

I recently left a city where all computer links to the airport had been accidentally severed by a construction crew. Flights were loading at least an hour late. Reservations were impossible, all boarding passes had to be manually reissued, and the arrivals and departure screens were out. In short, aviation at that city took a time trip back to the 1930s for nearly two days.

Other examples include the following: One virus knocked over 6,000 computers off the air, taking a number of administrative, transaction, and research networks with it. A major manufacturer found all of its programs suddenly being held hostage through a backdoor raid on the system. A major portion of this nation's long distance telephone service was shut down by poorly tested and deployed software, and a fire took out phone service in and around

Chicago along with a number of other networks that switched through the area as a hub.

To add to the impact, more and more enterprises are stretching their technology's capabilities to reach their processing goals. High transaction volumes, massive databases, and complex applications are all pushing many processing environments to their limits. Stable, well-controlled systems become absolute necessities in these circumstances.

More and more managers have suddenly found themselves owning or being charged with responsibilities for information processing systems. One of those responsibilities is the protection of the system and the information it contains. More to the point, the challenge is to make the system available for the business functions it supports while ensuring that the mission of the business is not damaged by a loss of data integrity.

The World of Information Protection

Information protection has many practitioners and commentators. Worldwide, there are a number of professional organizations and government and industry bodies with rules, laws, and regulations devoted to its care, feeding, growth, and proper upbringing. In spite of—or because of—this attention, there is still a fair amount of debate about what information protection is or, more accurately, what it includes.

Few definitions in this field are universally accepted or officially sanctioned. The ones I use in this book are in common use and, I hope, stated in straightforward English. Most important, they make sense. I've defined several of the most basic terms here, but all such words are defined in the Glossary. Throughout the book, you'll see these terms appear in **boldface** type the first time they are used in a chapter. Refer to the Glossary whenever you encounter one of these terms to refresh your memory as to its meaning for purposes of this book.

Information protection The prevention of, and recovery from, unauthorized disruption, modification, disclosure, or use of information and information resources, whether accidental or deliberate. Or, if you prefer a more positive statement, information protection is the preservation of the integrity, confidentiality, and availability of information and information resources.

There are many definitions of *information* in use today. A popular one is "data to which some judgment has been added." If you like it, use it. The issue of data versus information is not important for our purposes.

Most of the discussion in this book concentrates on information in electronic form, because technology has been the unwitting agent of many of the problems we face in protecting information in the 1990s. However, let me reiterate this important point: The more we depend on technology, the more we depend on people. Just think about how many people are involved in information processing where you work, shop, bank, travel, live, and relax. So although I concentrate on electronics, I can't ignore other forms of information that people use directly, such as hard copy and voice. It's silly to devote major resources to protecting computers and networks and let the same information pass around uncontrolled on the printed page or in conversation.

Information resources include information itself, computers and other processing hardware, software, telecommunications, and the related support infrastructure such as power, light, and air conditioning. But the most important information resource is people.

Information protection is usually subdivided into two general categories (see Figure I-1):

1. *Information security:* Maintaining the integrity of and controlling access to information and resources.

2. *Continuity:* Preventing, mitigating, and recovering from disruption. In this context, the terms *business resumption planning, disaster recovery planning,* and *contingency planning* may be used. Typically, these three terms concentrate on the recovery aspects of continuity. However, with the current dependency on information systems, even an hour's outage can inflict pain. So more time and energy are being shifted toward prevention and mitigation.

Control (as opposed to security and continuity) covers such things as data entry, design, procedure, and accounting errors. Some people distinguish between accuracy (error free) and integrity (tamper free), but even that distinction has opponents. Protection deals primarily with integrity, although I admit the line of demarcation is arbitrary. It's a subject of ongoing discussion among security professionals, auditors, systems designers, and managers. It becomes especially im-

Figure I-1. The components of information protection.

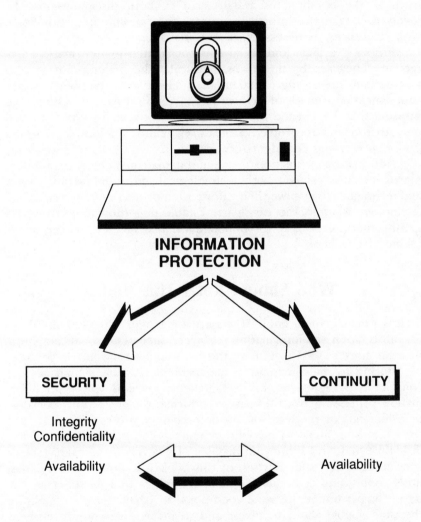

portant when you're talking about missions and responsibilities, but if you have responsibility for the entire system, it doesn't really matter what you call it.

Several other distinctions might be helpful. Information protection has a relation to, but is different from, *enterprise risk management,* which deals with such areas as criminal and terrorist activities, safety, protection of key executives, and insurance programs. Obviously, where overt physical threats to information resources are concerned (such as the bombing of a data center), both disciplines may be involved. I take the information protection viewpoint in this book, with references, as necessary, to risk management.

Privacy is a legal and social concept related to information protection. They are by no means identical. The major point of connection is in preserving confidentiality. There are a number of other issues such as primacy of privacy rights, physical eavesdropping, and invasion that are beyond the scope of this book. Privacy is addressed only as it relates to protective measures against disclosure or, if you prefer, preserving confidentiality.

Information protection is a general management responsibility. Managers must rely on both technological and administrative tools and techniques to achieve their information protection objectives. The technology is often the easy part. Establishing those objectives and getting there, especially for nontechnical management, is the major theme of this book.

Who Should Read This Book

This is a management book. If you are a manager with responsibilities for information and information resources, such as personal computers or even more powerful systems, this is the book for you. Or you may be aspiring to management, a management student, a management consultant, or a teacher of management. Perhaps you're an information processing practitioner, an information protection specialist, or a member of the legal or law-enforcement professions.

One thing all of us have in common is too much to do and too little time to do it. I share your problem; I'm a very active management consultant. The major portion of this book was written in airplanes, hotel rooms, and at home at odd hours and in odd bursts. You may be reading it under the same conditions, so I have tried to minimize the time you're about to invest and to make sure your investment pays off.

What This Book and the Author Have to Offer

In a few words, this book provides useful, practical, feasible advice on managing your information resources in a safer, more stable manner. The objective behind an information protection program is to enable, not to inhibit. The purpose of safety is to allow you to continue to operate, grow, and prosper. Information protection specialists, if they're doing their jobs correctly and effectively, should be instilling confidence, not scaring you out of your wits.

I once had a serious argument with a corporate lawyer who thought his job consisted of giving internal clients long lists of reasons why whatever they wanted to do was illegal (and occasionally immoral and fattening). His concept of completed staff work was an overwhelming list of exposures and risks. He believed his job ended where it really should have begun. I insisted that he was in business to tell me, as best he could, how I could reach my objective legally, not deluge me with reasons why I couldn't get there from here. I needed guidance, not impediments.

The same principle applies to information protection. Safeguarding information resources by making them actually or virtually unusable is not acceptable. Saying no and throwing body blocks at new programs protects nothing. We all know that most managers will opt for a higher level of risk rather than abandon what looks like a profitable program.

The primary purpose of an information security program is to *enable* only authorized persons and processes to do only what they are authorized to do. Everyone and everything else should be inhibited. But in the process of enabling authorized people to perform their functions, the security system should not require them to jump through hoops or perform "unnatural acts." It should enable.

The trick to making information security effective and palatable is to properly describe and relate those authorized persons and activities. This takes intelligent business decision making, judgment, and common sense. The information protection program has to support the organization's overall goals and objectives by supporting the goals and objectives of the information systems. Those goals and objectives aren't always obvious or clearly articulated. An interesting side effect of some protection programs I've worked on has been a clearer understanding by management of what and how their information resources contribute to their business or institution.

Before deciding to write this book, I looked at several current bibliographies on information protection. By and large, the works fall into two categories:

1. Specialty books and articles written by specialists primarily for professionals in the fields of security, contingency, technology, law enforcement, or ethics.

2. General readership discussions on computer crime and ethics.

There is a short bibliography at the end of this book to help you take advantage of some of these other works.

I have written articles of both varieties, but this work is intended to be something else (although it will deal with some of the same subjects). Although I have specialist's credentials, I can claim another credential that I hope will make this book different and useful to you—the manager's viewpoint. Between IBM and Deloitte & Touche, I have spent twenty-seven of my thirty-four working years as a manager in sales, systems engineering, development, marketing and sales promotion, human resources, government, and external relations—and in information protection. So when it comes to business management, I am much more of an active practitioner than a theoretician.

This book, then, is written with a manager's frame of reference and with a constant awareness that *information protection is not your primary objective.* It may not even rank in your top ten. However, it is something that you, as a manager, will probably have to deal with.

Not all of information protection involves crisis avoidance. A well-organized information protection program can and often does result in increased efficiency and productivity. Information protection is too frequently promoted through scare tactics. In this book, threats are put in perspective and stress is put on good management practice and the direct benefits that can result.

How to Use This Book

I hope you'll read this book in its entirety and in sequence. It has a logical progression, and some concepts and suggestions in the later chapters make more sense after exposure to the concepts and suggestions from earlier chapters. However, I'm realistic enough to know that all of us keep texts like this around for "reference under pressure"—the "give me some good words to answer this memo from the Audit Committee" phenomenon. So to help with those needs, each chapter has a summary describing its contents and organization and is written to stand as independently as possible. All important terms are defined in the Glossary and appear in bold type at their first use in each chapter. This structure should help you if you have long periods between reading sessions.

Understanding the Subject

1

What Is Information Protection, and Why Should You Care?

What's in this chapter?

- IP: Its Place in Business and in Systems Planning and Design
- How Can IP Contribute to Your Performance as a Manager?

The manager's dilemma in securing technology-based **information resources** is that some, but not all, **security** comes from procedures and technologies that, in turn, limit a system's productivity by reducing speed, access, user-friendliness, or scope. The trick to an effective and efficient **information protection** (IP) program is to provide the highest level of protection that is consistent with your requirements for productivity and cost-effectiveness. A guard dog that can distinguish between the good guys and the bad guys may be a good security investment, but the first time you get bitten yourself, you may rethink the dog's value. I go into this decision process more thoroughly in Chapters 3, 7, and 8.

IP: Its Place in Business and in Systems Planning and Design

Even if you work for a somewhat formalized and structured enterprise, the chances are only about 50-50 that you have a formal job description. Within that 50 percent, the chances are even smaller that you have a copy of your job description, and smaller still that you are being measured against it. The chance that IP is included as one of the job requirements against which you will be measured is practically zero.

On the other hand, the fact that you're reading this book suggests that your responsibility for protecting **information** has surfaced in some way—a query or command from senior management, an appointment to a task force, an audit, or (God forbid) an incident. Or perhaps, as an exemplary member of the management community, you just want to stay current with new business requirements. Whatever the reasons, let's try to increase your understanding and comfort index with IP.

To get some perspective on the place of IP in business, let's start out with a more basic question. What is the role of information and information **systems** (IS) in your organization? Again, since you're reading this, it is more than likely that information usage has become a very basic part of the management and operation of your organization. If you analyze many service organizations, you'll find that their entire operation consists of creating, processing, storing, and transmitting information. Just about the entire financial services industries group—banking, brokerage, insurance, credit services—fits that description. Even those that supply a more tangible service like transportation are highly dependent on information resources.

It's getting increasingly difficult to find any type of organization, business or otherwise, that does not demonstrate an increasing dependence on timely, accurate, complete, and appropriate information. Unfortunately, many organizations don't see information resources in the same light as they see the other resources they depend on. Somehow, the information process seems more transparent and is, therefore, taken for granted. This happens even though the enterprise may be spending the largest percentage of its budget on IS and can be stopped dead in its tracks if the information infrastructure fails. Information systems have a sort of public utility aspect to them in many managers' eyes. Like water or electricity, you just flip a switch or turn a spigot and it's there. This attitude is a partial carryover from the days when the management information systems (MIS) department and the data center supplied, for better or worse, most of the managers' and users' information needs.

Now, with distributed systems, local area networks (LANs), workstations, and personal computers (PCs), more of that information resource belongs directly to you and managers like you. Although that gives you a great deal of freedom, it also imposes more responsibility. Now, if you flip the switch and nothing is there or you don't like what comes out, the problem is often yours to fix.

To deal effectively with the problems that can arise from IS ownership, you have to plan for them. This is the major purpose of this book:

> To help you move IP from the ignore, react, and retrofit mode to the strategize, plan, and anticipate mode.

How Can IP Contribute to Your Performance as a Manager?

I mentioned above that very few managers' job descriptions mention IP as an item against which their performance will be specifically measured or rewarded. It may be implicit in the general management responsibilities we all carry in addition to the more specific goals, such as increase sales by 20 percent, reduce product cost by 10 percent, finish the development project 5 percent under budget and two months ahead of schedule.

You seldom find explicit protection goals because explicit information protection goals are difficult to describe. Unlike sales or costs or schedules, there is no convenient unit of measurement by which to communicate goals and objectives. What does a 10 percent increase in IP mean? It's difficult to determine whether you've done a great job or been lucky. If security violations are down 10 percent from last year, is it because of the security program, or has something happened to the reporting system? Are reduced violations a good index of safety? You've heard the same question asked about crime statistics.

Most senior managers, if they view it at all, view IP as a maintenance function—something that needs to be done and done well—but not a mainline contributor to achieving corporate goals and objectives. Some take a more negative view. At best, they regard IP as a necessary evil that diverts resources and attention from more productive activities. Recognize anyone?

If all this is true, it would seem that very few managers are going to be rocketed into the executive suite as a result of having an outstanding IP program. On the other hand, could you be rocketed into the street as a result of having a lousy one? Probably more likely.

Does that mean that IP programs are like Russian roulette? Is a "click" the best you can expect? Is there little upside potential but plenty of down? If so, should you figure out what the minimum investment must be to keep the auditors off your back and outright disasters from blowing you away and stop at that point? Not necessarily.

I'm not going to get tied up in a philosophical or political discussion on what constitutes "productive" activity in a business enterprise, but I do think you'll find that a number of productive side effects can result from increased attention to IP. Most of them come from increased stability and control.

The objective of a properly designed and implemented IP program should be to increase the stability and trustworthiness of your information systems so you can continue to grow your enterprise by increased and efficient use of your information resources. If your information resources are contributing to your performance as a manager, then stable, well-controlled, efficient, and effective information resources should make an even greater contribution to your performance.

Control is a very common word among managers. We use it in a number of ways. When I am in control, I perceive that as good. Someone else controlling me may not be so good. Most of us feel we are not as much in control as we want to be. On the other hand, many of us probably feel we are being overcontrolled by our management. We may see controls as too tight to achieve productivity. They may stifle creativity and innovation. However, when a business, department, or career goes under, loss of control is usually right at the top of the list of criticisms being laid on the culprit (or victim). It's a term about which we have ambivalent feelings, and appropriately so. Control, like freedom, can be overdone. The key to control is balance.

2

Changes in Information Processing Technology

What's in this chapter?

- Price-Performance
- Capacity and Function
- Modularity and Portability
- Applications
- Environments
- Organizations
- Extended Enterprises
- Laws, Regulations, and Standards

One of the characteristics that makes for a good consultant is the ability to listen. (God knows all of us can talk!) In planning our services, staffing, and strategies for our markets and in targeting our prospects and clients, we at Deloitte & Touche spend a lot of time and resources listening to our clients and potential clients and analyzing what they're telling us. One of the messages we've been getting loud and clear is the tremendous impact that changes in information processing have had on information-dependent organizations and the way they do business. From this, we've concluded that those same changes have also resulted in important, widespread, and subtly complex differences in how an organization controls and protects its **information resources.** Let's examine each area of change and examine some of the associated control implications.

I'm not going to catalog the seemingly endless improvements that are taking place in information processing technology. But I do want to categorize the eight major information processing characteristics that are creating new capabilities and challenges for modern business, government, education, medicine, and even the arts and religion. They all provide more opportunities for you as a manager to use information to improve your performance.

Price-Performance

Today you can carry under your arm and place under your desk processors and associated software that ten years ago would have needed a data center to support them.

Mass production, miniaturization, standardization, mass marketing, advanced software development techniques, and packaging have all contributed to the low-cost, high-powered processing we currently see at every level of hardware **platform**—mainframe, mini, and micro—and at every level of software as well. There is a very close similarity in design and implementation between current microcessor-based operating systems and the software that drives major mainframes. While processing power and capacity have been increasing, prices have been decreasing dramatically.

• *End result.* More processing power for less cost makes it possible to provide processing capabilities, often with astonishing function, to a much wider and diverse group of **information** users, most of whom have very little technical expertise.

• *Control implications.* The consequences are more users, decentralized controls, and greater power and complexity in the hands of more people. A fellow practitioner and friend of mine, Bob Courtney, calls it the democratization of information processing. Democracy always makes control more difficult. The trend, no doubt, will continue.

Capacity and Function

Regardless of price, today's technology has a tremendous potential for processing, storing, and transmitting immense amounts of data. Coupled with that capacity is extremely sophisticated function that can support complex and computation-intensive **applications**. The vast amount of data that can be stored on-line (measured in trillions of characters or more) is just a precursor of things to come. The speed with which those data can be processed is equally impressive.

• *End result.* We get more and more concentration of data and function in individual processors. At the same time, each processor is extending its reach through networking.

• *Control implications.* The greater the density of information in any particular processing point or node, the greater the potential impact of a failure or attack. The greater the speed of processing, the faster an error, attack, or anomaly can degenerate into a serious failure or out-of-control situation. Obviously, the converse is also true. The extra capacity and function can also be employed to enhance protective measures.

Modularity and Portability

We are moving toward a technological state where an increasing number of functional units, especially storage devices, processing units, and communications modules, can be transferred from base system to base system. Data can be moved, reconfigured, modified, upgraded, and replicated with ease; so too can entire processing environments.

• *End result.* The relationship between hardware and data, already tenuous, will become even more fluid. The relationship between one hardware unit and another will become equally loose, and the transportability of function from module to module, environment to environment, owner to owner, and user to user will become very simple indeed.

• *Control implications.* Physical protection and restriction will no longer be feasible in the same sense as we understood it in the days of highly stationary mainframes and smaller processors. On the other hand, physical protection will become (is becoming) a much more critical part of information resource protection. When an individual can walk off with a major processing module, storage device, or database in a pocket or handbag, the protection game has to be played differently.

Applications

Even though price-performance, processing power, capacity, portability, and modularity may all be greatly enhanced, the value to the user and the enterprise must still be measured in terms of enhanced applications. If you can't translate all of this power and capacity into useful activity, technology for its own sake fades very rapidly as a motivator. However, at the rate new applications are being developed and deployed at all levels, there doesn't seem to be too much danger of that happening.

Look at microprocessors, for example. It isn't unusual to find these devices being used for multimedia presentations, artificial intelligence, desktop publishing, statistical analysis, database functions, word processing, spreadsheet, computer-aided design, transaction processing, project management, network management, electronic mail, and entertainment. That's not bad for a small device costing a few thousand dollars. In the mini and mainframe range, the application base can include all of the enterprise's essential business functions.

• *End result.* An increasing number of organizations have passed the point of no return in relying on information processing systems to carry on their critical business functions—that is, those activities that support the fundamental purposes and objectives of the organization.

• *Control implications.* The computer is no longer simply a record-keeping or number-crunching device. It has become a major operational component in most enterprises. Therefore, the control and safety of technology-based applications and information resources can have a significant effect on the well-being of the enterprise.

Environments

As a result of micros and minis being used at departmental and individual levels, more than half of the processing power in most medium to large organizations may be found outside the data centers and often outside the control of the enterprise's management information systems (MIS) organization. That statement doesn't mean that over half of the *critical applications* have gone outside MIS. For immediate future at least, I believe that the preponderance of them still belong to MIS and are mainframe based. So don't take the mainframe dinosaur stories too seriously. Mainframes, MIS, and data centers will be around for quite a while. *But their roles are changing and they're no longer the only game in town.* Those are very important differences.

Therefore, it is becoming increasingly likely that major business applications may have to rely on information resources in uncontrolled or hostile environments. A hostile environment is one in which you must assume a high likelihood of some undesirable event happening unless you exercise some deliberate controls to prevent it. Automatic teller machines are assumed to be in hostile environments both because of where they are and what they are. Most portable microprocessors should be considered as being in hostile environments. **Systems** in open office, factory, or warehouse space may be in hostile environments. Cellular phones, radio frequency transceivers, and similar devices used by route salespeople, service people, and other individuals on call are often in hostile environments. Electronic mail processors, fax rooms, stand-alone faxes, file servers, and shared systems may all be in hostile space.

- *End result.* By making the information resources of an enterprise more available and widespread, we are subjecting them to a higher level of potential attack, accident, misuse, or failure. It's part of the price of flexibility and exploiting new technologies and applications.
- *Control implications.* By realistically assessing the inherent threats and vulnerabilities and considering control alternatives, management can arrive at a more acceptable level of environmentally induced risk, often without curtailing the desired flexibility. Conversely, management may decide that flexibility isn't worth the risk.

Organizations

One of the more subtle but potent changes that information processing systems have helped create are new organizational structures and relationships. In mergers and acquisitions, the success or failure of the organizational marriage often depends on the ability of the partners to communicate in their merged state. This applies at every level, and at whatever state of autonomy the merger envisioned.

Even in organizations that depend on information flow to meet their business objectives—indeed, in some cases in which information flow *is* their business—the planning for information processing and flow in the merged state is inadequately thought through. Oddly, many of these mergers and acquisitions would not have been possible without telecommunications, process and data interchange and distribution, and some common technical architectures and platforms. The same may be true if an enterprise divests itself of a unit or units.

• *End result.* Integration at the functional and organizational level is often delayed at great expense and sometimes loss of competitive advantage. The structure envisioned under the terms of the merger or acquisition may prove impossible, unlikely, or too expensive. Confusion, infighting, lack of clear direction, and loss of key personnel may result. Goals may not be met.

• *Control implications.* If the information process comes up short, the control structure usually comes up shorter, placing the resulting systems, applications, and networks in a state of potential jeopardy, which may further aggravate the problems of the merged entity. One financial services organization I know, in the third year of its merged state, still suffers from serious instability in its networks. It need not be so.

Extended Enterprises

Probably the most significant result of the movement of information processing to distributed environments through networking is the development of the "extended enterprise." In its simplest form, the extended enterprise is the common community of information systems users, owners, and process suppliers resulting from the development of a network of mutually advantageous applications and data resources. Think for a moment about a number of organizations tied together through an electronic funds transfer (EFT) system or engaged in mutual transaction processing through electronic data interchange (EDI) conventions. At a more basic level, consider a group of microprocessor users loosely tied to each other through an electronic mail or bulletin board system. That system extends beyond any single organization to which the family of users may belong. That's the extended enterprise.

• *End result.* The result is a series of relationships, policies, standards, and procedures that transcend any one participating organization. The information processing entities must be cognizant of their processing partners as they make decisions that may directly or indirectly affect them. The landscape changes technically, operationally, and often legally. Responsibilities become more complex and transcend the traditional self-interest of the single enterprise.

• *Control implications.* The safety of the processing partner becomes a more dominant factor in information protection practices.

The virus as a security issue has gotten a great deal of attention in the past few years. The virus can be a very destructive form of attack on information systems, destroying large quantities of software and data and disabling networks of individual processors in the act.

In examining the virus threat with clients and prospective clients, there is a sameness to the pattern of the discussions. It usually starts with the question, "How can we defend against and recover from a virus attack?" A fair and appropriate question, which we usually discuss at some length. We examine all of the network connections, software sources and individuals that could carry potential virus attacks.

Somewhere in the course of the discussion, I usually ask, "What are you doing to avoid being the cause of a virus attack on your processing partners? What legal, contractual, or relationship exposures would you face? Can you afford to be the cause—probably unwitting— of knocking your best client or distributors off the air for an extended period?" The response is frequently dead silence.

Technology has enabled most enterprises to move electronically beyond their own walls, environment, locale, country, and region. The responsibilities associated with that expansion are just beginning to surface. Many of those responsibilities can be addressed by increased attention to controls.

Laws, Regulations, and Standards

As a final illustration of the changing environment that has been presented to us by information technology, let's briefly look at the legal environment that has resulted. It is by no means clear, consistent, or even logical. Listed below are a few areas in which local, state or provincial, national, and international laws, standards, or agreements have been passed that bear on information and information technology usage. The following are being enforced with varying degrees of vigor:

• Personal privacy
• Computer crime

- National security
- Environmental protection
- Occupational health and safety
- Fair credit practices
- Fair employment practices and labor relations
- Copyright and intellectual property rights
- Telecommunications law
- Libel and defamation
- Freedom of information
- Freedom of speech
- Financial disclosure and generally accepted accounting practices
- Insider trading and other securities regulations

There are more but I'm sure you get the picture. Many of these issues didn't exist before the advent of information processing technology. Others have existed since the beginning of recorded law. All of them have been affected and changed by technological advances. As a manager, you too can be affected.

- *End result.* The constraints of information-related laws and regulations have become more directly important to the line manager. Along with all of your other concerns, your awareness in this area needs to be broadened and sharpened.
- *Control implications.* Not only you but all of the information owners and users who report to you have legal responsibilities you may not have previously realized.

So where does this leave you? If you stopped reading right here, did nothing, changed nothing, you might go on indefinitely without any noticeable effect. But I don't trust the odds on doing nothing. Subsequent chapters give you the basis for some realistic, cost-effective, individually tailored measures that will help you enhance your **information protection** status without turning your managerial world upside down.

3

What Are You Protecting?

What's in this chapter?

- Information: Your Greatest Asset
  —How Information Differs From Other Assets
  —The Value of Information
- Controlling Access to Information
  —Classifying Information
  —Risk Management
  —Determining Criticality

The first thing we need to discuss is whether you and your organization consider **information** to be an "asset" at all. I don't necessarily mean that it appears in your financial statement as such (although, depending on the nature of your enterprise, that could be true). What I'm really asking is whether there is a conscious understanding that information can be (and often is) more valuable to the success of your organization than most tangible assets such as plant and equipment. In fact, in many organizations, only the people are more valuable. But even then, much of the value assigned to a work force is based on what they know—skills and experience.

Information: Your Greatest Asset

If you believe that information is a special form of asset, then several lines of action logically follow. The first step is to begin treating information as similar, but not identical, to other enterprise assets.

15

There are many obvious similarities between the conventional plant, equipment, and raw material and the information you use. In fact, information may be both the raw material and the finished product—it certainly is in many of the financial services and communications industries. But no matter what your product or service, you use information to produce your end product, establish customer relations, create sales, develop products and services, track and report results, and manage and grow the business. Without it, you'd be deaf, dumb, and blind in the marketplace.

How much time do today's enterprises dedicate to growing and using information? Judging from the usage figures on computers, software, and information-related services, quite a lot. How much time do they spend protecting information? From every study I've seen, not nearly enough.

How Information Differs From Other Assets

What makes information different from other assets? Realistically, there are limits to how far you can go in trying to apply your tangible asset perspectives to that great intangible—information. In fact, that is the major point of difference. Information is intangible, and it's becoming more so as it becomes less reliant on a specific medium for transmission and preservation. Before the advent of electronics, most information was transmitted either intangibly through conversation or by some tangible means such as a book or document. But those days are either gone forever or rapidly disappearing. Today, information is no longer *permanently* connected to its medium, but is transiently represented by magnetic pulses on a disk, screen, or transmission line. Documentation does not always mean a document. It can mean an electronic file. That file, in its entirety, may never appear in printed form.

The important point is that in its transient, electronic state, information is much more susceptible to copying, proliferation, modification, disclosure, destruction, and uncontrolled usage than it was in printed or punched card form, where the medium and the message had a much higher level of interdependency.

Electronics also makes it more difficult to firmly establish and maintain ownership and authorship. How often have you received information in electronic form; added to, subtracted from, or otherwise modified it; merged it with other data; and performed any number of information processing functions on it? At what point did the data cease being someone else's and start being yours? If we were talking about equipment you had purchased and then modified to perform a certain function, you'd probably be able to point to the line of demarcation between its original and altered states. But it's not so easy with a database that has multiple contributors and owners. Often, ownership of information becomes a somewhat arbitrary business decision based less on actual ownership rights and more on business requirements.

Ownership, as used in **information protection** circles, means the right and obligation to determine who can use information, what they can do, and under what circumstances.

Another distinguishing characteristic of information as an asset is its sheer size. By comparison with your other business assets, information is probably much more variable and voluminous and may indeed be immeasurable. A single portable computer can store over a hundred million characters on its hard disk. Would you seriously consider taking a book or physical inventory of your information? Probably not! However, I strongly suggest that you consider at least a categorization and classification of the *types* of information you use in your enterprise. That, in itself, can be very revealing.

The Value of Information

What is your information worth? The answer is the crux of your whole information protection strategy. Obviously, as prudent managers, you want to dedicate only those resources that are necessary and appropriate to protect your information assets. You arrive at that figure by analyzing the cost and value of your information. This analysis involves two parts. You must ask:

1. What is the information worth to you? What do you use it for, and what does it contribute to meeting your business objectives, goals, and critical success factors?
2. What is it worth to a competitor, to the media, or to a hostile consumer advocate? Is the information you use truly proprietary?

Many organizations, once they begin to think of information in asset terms, become fanatic about proprietary information rights. I have heard many variations of the following statement from otherwise sophisticated business and governmental organizations: "All information used by the USGUYS Corporation is considered proprietary and must be treated as such by USGUYS employees." That statement should take care of establishing ownership, right? Wrong!

Although the motivation is right on target—let's protect our information assets—the viewpoint is misguided. Is all the information you use in the normal course of the business day really yours? I doubt it. Without considering the obvious ones like the phone book and the newspaper, ask yourself where the rest of your information assets actually came from. How much of it is public domain? How much came from other business sources such as vendors and contractors? How much do you share with your customers, suppliers, security analysts, and the public?

Can you establish a precise, monetary value for your information assets? I doubt it. And it isn't really necessary for your purposes. I haven't seen many organizations come up with precise figures that couldn't be questioned or restated. The reason for this imprecision is the *relative* value information has.

There's the question of time and occasion. If you're stuck in an airport, having a list of the available flights to your destination can be the most valuable information in the world. Most of the time, however, airline schedules make very dull reading. Getting the financial results of a publicly traded organization one day earlier than everyone else can be very advantageous (and probably illegal). The day after its publication, that same information is still valuable but on a different scale.

Then there's the question of value to whom? In the hands of a competitor, some of your information files could have devastating negative impact. Human resources and credit files can have varying degrees of importance based on who is using them and for what.

Finally, even the question of cost can be addressed differently. Do you value your information on the basis of original procurement or development cost, cost of replacement, or impact of loss? Each number can be dramatically different.

Precision isn't necessary to make the kinds of security decisions that will be discussed here. In fact, striving for precision can be counterproductive. The process of valuing information is subtle and needs careful management consideration.

The following characteristics are important for a successful and cost-effective information protection plan:

- *Rationality.* Don't ask people to do what they regard as impossible or silly—like locking up public phone books.

- *Appropriateness.* What is necessary for the Central Intelligence Agency probably doesn't apply to your company.
- *Cost-effectiveness.* If your countermeasures exceed the value of what you're protecting, you'd better rethink them.

Controlling Access to Information

The major purpose of an access control function in an organization is to ensure that only authorized people have access to only authorized information and, having gained access, that they can perform only authorized activities on it. There are two sides to the coin: (1) classification of the information and (2) authorization of users and related processes. The owner(s) of the data and the manager(s) of the users together establish the ground rules for access. Authorization of users is discussed in Chapter 9.

Classifying Information

You classify information and information resources in order to establish the appropriate levels of protective behavior toward those resources. The fundamental underlying assumption is that not all information is equally important to the enterprise.

That assumption may not apply in your case. If all your information is indeed equally important, then your job is simple. Pick a value to assign to the resources you want to protect. Use that value as an umbrella for determining how much you want to spend and on what you want to invest your protective dollars.

However, if like most organization managers you feel, at least intuitively, that some information is worth more than others, then at least a high-level attempt at classification is in order to ensure that you neither overspend nor underspend on protection; that what you do spend is properly directed; and that your information is getting appropriate protection for its value.

It's difficult (but not absolutely impossible) to develop an effective information protection program without some level of formal classification of information and information resources. An informal classification process that relies on common sense and knowledge of corporate culture and market sensitivity can carry an organization a long way toward the basics of physical protection. In most organizations, knowing what to lock up at night and what to send by bonded messenger is as much a function of common sense and awareness as it is of any formal set of rules.

When you start using a computer, one thing becomes obvious: Electronic devices and software are limited to the degree of common sense the designers saw fit to put into them, and that level is often quite low. Computers and most computer software are incredibly literal minded. They do what you tell them to—no more, no less. There is little or no common sense to interpret what you really meant. This means that as far as **security** is concerned, the value of information resources needs to be more carefully defined and transmitted to electronic systems in order for them to properly invoke their protective mechanisms on your behalf.

It is important to remember that information classification is a business decision process. Do not leave it entirely in the hands of the technicians or security specialists. They can help create the classification program, but the decisions belong with the managers running the business processes and applications.

The next step toward making that business decision is to look at your information resources in two modes:

1. *Security.* The need for confidentiality, integrity, and controlled usage.
2. *Availability.* Information that is there when you need it.

These are not interchangeable characteristics, and each may call for different protective measures.

Let's look at a couple of examples to illustrate the differences between security and availability. Human resources files may require a high level of confidentiality, but if you couldn't get into the medical records for several weeks, the chances are that nothing terrible would happen to the whole organization. (If we were talking about medical records in a hospital, the whole scenario would obviously change.) This is a case of information requiring high security—both confidentiality and integrity—and, depending on the employee's medical status, a variable demand for availability.

There are other types of information, particularly business transactions, that have, at best, a moderate need for confidentiality but a high requirement for integrity. In this case, the security and **control** measures must ensure that origination, modification, update, and destruction of the information are carefully controlled, with less emphasis on controlling "read-only" access.

Let's turn things around. An electronic library that supplies excerpts from the *Congressional Record* is dealing with material that is in the public domain, but it supplies the information on demand to a large number of users. Here we have a high availability requirement if the service is going to support the needs of its clients, but the information it supplies has a low confidentiality rating.

And remember, one of the most important elements in availability is the network: both sides of the network—voice and data. The vast majority of organizations I've dealt with in the past few years put *network* security and availability as number one or two in their priorities. Often, their voice nets have a higher priority than their data nets, especially if they depend on 800 or 900 number systems for order entry or customer service.

Obviously, there will also be information resources that have high security *and* availability requirements and some that have neither. Your job is to look at each major data file, **application,** and its related information resources in terms of availability and security.

The next step is to establish classification categories and criteria for confidentiality, integrity, and availability that:

- Are based on business impact,
- Can be clearly and consistently interpreted by your managers and information **systems** technicians, and
- Will result in different protective actions for each category.

All of these points are important. If the difference between two types of data isn't important to your business from a security or availability standpoint, don't include it. Make the language as uncomplicated and the categories as intelligible as possible. Try the categories out on different groups of managers and see if they come up with the same perceptions and results you do.

Keep the number of categories to an irreducible minimum. If two categories don't require substantially different treatment, combine them. In most circumstances, I believe that three or four categories should suffice for most business organizations.

Probably the most common mistake is borrowing someone else's categories. By all means, capitalize on other people's experience and efforts, but do not adopt a set of classifications simply on the prestige of the source, even when they're in the same industry sector as your firm. Use the following as an example—but that's all.

The USGUYS Corporation (and its southern subsidiary, USFOLKS) is a manufacturer of high-tech communications-related gear, primarily for home and small-business usage—phones, faxes, small computers, small copiers, and support devices. It has reviewed its information resources and has concluded that for purposes of security and avail-ability, it needs four categories for confidentiality, three for integrity, and three for availability. Therefore, each data file, application, and supporting information resource will carry one (of four) confidentiality classification, one (of three) integrity classification, and one (of three) availability classification.

[If this sounds like a lot of categories, remember the fundamental consideration. For each category, you are going to supply a mean-ingfully different level of protection. If you find out that two cate-gories of confidentiality or integrity end up with the same set of protective measures, combine them. Or if you think you can use the same protective measures to provide both integrity and confi-dentiality, combine them and call it security. This is not supposed to be a definitional hair-splitting exercise. It's supposed to optimize the time and expense you commit to protecting your information.

Try the categories on some managers who have ownership responsibilities for the information. If they can't adequately distin-guish between one category and another in terms of importance or what they want done differently with each class, cut back on the categories or improve the definitions. Back to our example.]

The confidentiality categories are:

1. *Highly confidential.* This covers a small number of files in-cluding new product designs and business planning data, pricing, customer credit files, vendor selection criteria, and those financial applications that, if improperly disclosed, could result in very signif-icant strategic or financial damage to the company, its clients, or its vendors. Some executive correspondence belongs here.

Such files are carefully restricted on a "need-to-know" basis to a very small number of users. Accessibility depends on whether that person needs to know that information in order to do his or her job. Users are individually restricted in what they can and cannot see and copy. Logs are kept of all accesses. Second-person sign-off may be necessary for many transactions.

All physical files are kept locked and all keys strictly accounted for. Electronic files are under a stringent access control system. Transmission is carried out under highly controlled circumstances and may include encryption, restricted telephone lines, or bonded couriers. Careful audit and controls are maintained on the levels and extent of access privilege granted.

This category probably constitutes less than 10 percent of US-GUYS' information resources.

2. *Confidential.* These are files that could cause serious damage to the company if disclosed contrary to management's wishes, but to a lesser extent than the category above. Most financial transactions below a certain dollar level, human resources, payroll, customer lists, marketing performance, and most executive correspondence belong here. Production data, engineering data on current product lines, and process engineering belong here. Separation of duties and second-person sign-off may apply.

All physical files are kept locked. Usage is restricted, but to a lesser degree than the highly confidential category. The same types of physical and electronic safety measures are used, but the restrictions allow somewhat broader access privileges. Audit is done on a periodic spot-check basis. Lower-level transmission protection such as file compression techniques or registered mail may be used.

Less than 20 percent of USGUYS' information resources belongs here.

3. *Internal use only.* This covers information that most prudent business managers would rather keep inside the company even though the damage caused by disclosure might not be very serious. Access is generally granted to individuals as a result of their job descriptions or department membership and the fact that they are employees in good standing.

The criteria for inclusion in this category are usually strongly conditioned by the corporate culture and labor relations. If the organization is "one big happy family," this category is usually a rather open and loosely controlled one. If there have been problems in the past, this category may be a good deal tighter. If the industry is highly competitive and industrial espionage is rampant, much of the information normally put in this category may get folded into the one above.

Measurement of the potential damage requires a review of the entire processing, storage, and transmission environment, including the nature of the business and its environment. The same type of data may not necessarily be classified the same way from enterprise to enterprise because of these other conditions.

Generally, this category encompasses 50 percent or more of USGUYS' information resources.

4. *Unclassified (or a similar term).* This applies to material in the public domain or that has no, or extremely low, potential for damage through disclosure, modification, or misuse. This final 20 percent of USGUYS' information may range from public telephone books and cafeteria menus through publicly available news services and the like. This is not the easiest category to define. Some companies refer to it as "All Other," but may or may not put the same things in it. For example, some companies are very careful about their internal phone books; others publish them to the world.

This category does not mean no protection. It means baseline protection. For example, the company may have already decided that all mainframe computers, software, and associated storage and transmission devices will be subject to physical and logical protection commensurate with their own inherent value. Any data residing on those systems, therefore, gets the same level of baseline protection.

A similar set of rules may apply to microprocessors, fax rooms, telephone cabinets, private branch exchanges (PBXs), licensed software, and the like. The related resources are treated to the same level of baseline protection.

In using this category, don't simply make it the default after all other choices have been rejected. Consider, instead, whether the baseline protective measures, if any, are sufficient to protect this information.

Next on USGUYS' list is *integrity.* Here, the company is concerned with unauthorized modification. Disclosure may still be important, but the level of concern here may be higher or lower.

Analogous to the need-to-know concept dealing with confidentiality is the "level of least privilege." It means that people can create, modify, update, or destroy only that information that is essential to performing their jobs. This concept carries over to programmers and others who can affect the process. It can be overdone, but it is a necessary approach to achieve high levels of integrity.

USGUYS' three categories for integrity are as follows.

1. *Highly restricted modification.* Unauthorized creation or modification of these data can cause significant damage to the enterprise,

its customers, vendors, associates, or the public. These types of data require individual authorization by the data owner for specific activities on specific data fields (views), records, and files. For example, only certain individuals may initiate changes to the executive compensation program. Formula or bill of materials changes may fall here. If USGUYS were a hospital, patient medication lists and lists of individuals authorized to dispense medicines would apply. Credit ratings and personnel files may belong here or in the next category.

Not only are the data controlled, but so are all processes that affect the data, such as software programs. The rationale is that if someone can change the program itself, that person may be able to do more damage than if he or she had transactional access to the data.

Again, we are probably talking about 10 percent of USGUYS' data, but it may not be the same 10 percent that was highly restricted for confidentiality.

2. *Restricted modification.* Potential for moderate damage through fraud, electronic pilferage, or other forms of unauthorized personal gain is included here. This classification applies to data for which the enterprise is willing to grant modification rights on a restricted-group basis. For example, all members of the accounts payable department can perform certain classes of transactions on certain classes of data (but not necessarily all transactions on all classes of data). Some groups may be authorized to enter new information but not to alter existing records.

If the industry or company has a high incidence of fraud, embezzlement, physical loss, or hijacking, this category may not even exist; all the items normally found here may be placed in the more restrictive classification.

Once again, there may be a wider "read-only" audience. This may be about 40 to 50 percent of USGUYS' data.

3. *Controlled modification.* This one deals with information resources that you would probably let any employee in good standing make changes to under appropriate circumstances. Individuals may be allowed to alter internal directories and schedules relating to themselves. Outside vendors and customers may have access under this category or the category above.

There are not a lot of data in this classification, and usually there are no such things as data that anyone can modify uncontrolled. In short, you usually keep a tighter rein on integrity issues than you do on confidentiality.

Last, let's talk about USGUYS' *availability* categories:

1. *Critical availability.* This means that these are the bedrock data files, applications, and transactions that are critical to the business function. If these are unavailable for even a short period, serious business or organizational consequences will occur—maybe even failure. For USGUYS, this may be 20 percent or less of their information.

These types of data differ widely, depending on the nature of the business or organization. If an airline loses its reservation system for even a short period, it could suffer severe losses on its competitive routes. If a law-enforcement or emergency-response network goes out for even a few minutes, the results could be very serious. If a patient-monitoring system goes out for a few seconds, the results could be fatal. On the other hand, some organizations can have their data processing go out for days or weeks and keep on going.

I use the term *meantime to pain* several times in this book. It's an easy concept to work with. How long before it hurts? How much does it hurt? Equally important, but often overlooked, is what does it take to recover? Another frequently used term for this is *maximum allowable downtime.*

2. *High availability.* This means that the application, data files, or transactions listed under this classification are necessary to the continued operation of the organization but are not in the same critical category as those classified above. You may also include under this category those applications and files that turn critical periodically, such as at the end of the month, quarter, or year. This category of information makes up about 50 percent.

3. *Other availability.* This classification can be called any number of things. Regardless of title, it implies that the enterprise can go for a considerable period without these particular information resources or can find alternative processing modes (often pencil and paper) to work around the outage. In the USGUYS example, this category would probably be 30 percent or more.

Risk Management

A point that may be overlooked is that this whole classification process is part of **risk management.** The **recovery** or preventive strategy that you bring to bear on these applications should reflect not only the availability requirements for the particular information resources but also the degree of risk you are willing to take with respect to them.

Many texts, articles, and consultants often make **risk assessment** out to be a rather scientific process based on probabilities, risks, and impacts. There is much to be said for the process. The problem is that in most organizations another element kicks in very early and often alters the results dramatically. That element is *available budget.*

We'd all like to believe that, faced with the inherent risks associated with information protection, top management will immediately respond with an influx of all the necessary funds to make the integrity and availability of the information resources a number-one priority. The fact is that more often than not, faced with the risks associated with information protection, top management will indeed respond, but seldom to the extent we desire. So if you have some feeling for what budget allocation will or won't fly, try to get that confirmed early in the program.

That doesn't mean you should shortchange the classification or risk assessment program because you can't afford the measures you might need. Get the risks and classifications defined. Then, any plan you develop should anticipate an initial shortfall and a multiyear buildup of protective and recovery activities. If you're in a budget crunch, don't go for all or nothing. You'll get nothing.

Determining Criticality

Let's outline some fundamental principles for determining criticality:

• This can be a very political process. No one wants to admit that they and their departments are not critical to the business. Make sure the people you are talking to understand that you are not making an overall value judgment on their department's worth. What you are trying to do is determine whether and for how long they and the business can continue to operate without information processing resources. It is a difficult question, and getting the terminology straight can avoid a lot of hostility and misunderstanding.

• Not every application within a critical business function is, in itself, critical. Too many analyses of criticality tend to stop at the business function level: Customer service is critical, therefore all customer service applications are critical. I doubt it.

- Measure criticality on two time scales:

    1. Tolerable period of outage
    2. Tolerable period to overcome a backlog of transactions

The transaction backlog after an outage is restored can often be a killer. If you are using an information facility at or near capacity twenty-four hours a day, your time for backlog elimination may be infinite. Replacing hardware or software may be the easy part. Managing the backlog to zero may not be so easy.

- Some applications in noncritical business functions may become critical because of their relationship to other critical functions and applications. When you designate a specific application or information resource as critical, trace its origins, relationships, and dependencies and treat those resources and applications as part of the critical application.

- Finally, these are business decisions you are making. There is technical content, of course, but don't frame your thinking around specific hardware, software, or processing environments. Think in terms of business processes. You may find, for instance, that some of the most critical business functions have a relatively low computing and communications content. Don't stop there. Think in terms of the people dependencies that probably exist in those functions. What happens if they can't get to work or there is no place for them to work? If they're critical, say so.

If this is your first attempt at classification, try not to make a big production number out of it. Some organizations set up massive committees that agonize and debate over each subcategory and criterion. That sort of precision may be necessary if you are trying to develop the definitive dictionary of security and **continuity** terminology. But you're not. You're trying to get a set of workable indices that will provide a platform for protective and productive decision making. Anything that goes beyond that is waste of your efforts and resources.

Try your classification schemes out early on the managers and information workers who will have to live with them. A friend of mine uses a variation on the old "proof of the pudding" adage: "After all the lab work and market studies, the dog food is marketable only if the dogs will eat it." Make the scheme fit your organization and be specific about what measures you want carried out under each category, including manual protective measures.

Information resources are the focal point, and the protective program should address each situation in which those resources will be used, including outside the organization.

4

Who and What Are You Protecting Against?

The goal of **information protection** is to preserve the integrity, confidentiality, and availability of **information.** The fundamental threats that may keep you from attaining this goal are unauthorized disruption, disclosure, modification, or use of information and **information resources,** whether accidental or deliberate.

The first term to focus on is *unauthorized.* Although it's difficult to think of an authorized disruption—scheduled maintenance of equipment or software might fit—it is certainly reasonable to think in terms of authorized disclosure, modification, and use. In fact, if you couldn't do those things, your information **system** wouldn't be of much use to you. But authorized by whom? For the moment, let's say that enterprise management is the authorizing power.

The important point is that enterprise management must enunciate in a statement of policy or similar communication what its intentions are regarding the use and protection of information and information resources. These should be further explained through standards, procedures, and guidelines.

If such an explicit structure doesn't exist in your organization, you are not alone. Organizations with clear, written information protection policies, standards, and procedures are still in the minority. In fact, the number of businesses without formal policies and standards of any type is amazingly high. This is probably a throwback to a time when the organization was smaller, more directly managed, and more flexible in what it could or could not do. Many managers equate policies and standards with that cursed scourge—bureaucracy. But written standards and policies can often help reduce bureaucracy by clearly stating what is and is not appropriate.

Even in the absence of a formal policy and standards program, the odds are pretty good that if you and your fellow managers were to sit down for a few hours you could come up with a set of statements that summarized the practices of your organization. Whether formally stated or, more likely, passed on through general practice, corporate culture, and folklore, you probably have some generally accepted concepts about what constitutes appropriate behavior toward information.

The phrase *whether accidental or deliberate* also warrants explanation. In this age of hackers and viruses, it's easy to forget that many of the most damaging events affecting information resources are the result of plain old ordinary mistakes. We get into a gray area here. What about the basic accuracy of the data or the process that uses it? What about the incompetent programmer, operations technician, or data-entry clerk? The difference between quality and **security** is often in the eye of the beholder.

Threats to Your Information's Security

Now, let's concentrate on the threats themselves. If the unauthorized disruption, disclosure, modification, or use is accidental and results from poor design, implementation, or operation, it's a protection issue. Otherwise, it's generally a quality or **control** issue, which is related, but not the same.

Disruption

Disruption is sometimes described as *loss of service*. The converse of this threat is availability or **continuity.** The information and information resources must be there when, where, in the manner, and to the degree you want them.

The class of disruptive threats that usually comes to mind first is physical or environmental. For example:

- Fire
- Falling water (rain, leaks from other sources)
- Rising water or flooding (rising and falling water are dealt with differently)
- Explosion
- Earthquake
- Toxic substances
- Structural failure (from whatever cause, e.g., snow, wind, fatigue)
- Infrastructural failure
  —Power
  —Light
  —Water
  —HVAC (Heating, Ventilation, Air Conditioning)
  —Access (e.g., elevators)
  —Telecommunications
  —Transportation

The next group of disruptive threats deals with the way people act:

- Strikes or lockouts
- Vandalism and other criminal attacks on persons or property
- Loss of critical personnel
- War
- Legal prohibition
- Operational errors or omissions

The next group is less frequently addressed, but I believe these areas are becoming the most prevalent forms of information resource disruption. They deal with the *logical* outage. By logical, I mean related to the technological process, usually program-based. The opposite of *logical* as it is used here is *physical,* not *illogical.* They include:

- Programming error
- Hardware or software design error

- Virus attack
- Hacking
- Time bombs, Trojan horses, and other forms of deliberate programming-based attacks
- Nonphysical telecommunications error (often programming caused)

Outages (service disruptions) of all kinds share common characteristics that are of interest in planning any kind of a protection program. For example:

1. The nature of the damage
2. The extent of the damage
3. The operational, technical, and business impact of the damage
4. Available alternatives
5. The cost of **recovery** and **restoration**
6. The time required for recovery and restoration

The term *recovery*, as I'm using it here, means the state when the information processing functions are *operational* again. *Restoration*, on the other hand, means that everything is back to normal, including cleaning up the backlog of transactions that may have been processed in an alternative mode. Recovery may come rather quickly. Restoration may take much longer.

Let's examine these characteristics one by one:

1. *The nature of the damage.* If the damage is physical, such as fire, water, or toxic contamination, the problem is dramatically different from, say, a loss of power due to a brief public utility failure. In the latter case, your primary concern is alternative action until the resource is back on line. The rest is the power company's problem. If your system is a smoldering hulk, the result is the same—you're out of action—but the problem is bigger and it's yours to solve in its entirety.

2. *The extent of the damage.* A fire that guts an entire data center is a lot different from one that destroys a power supply in a microprocessor. A flood may be messy and temporarily disruptive, or it may leave you without any usable information resources.

3. *The operational, technical, and business impact of the damage.* In the final analysis, this is the most important question. How serious is

the outage, especially from the standpoint of being able to carry on the business or organizational functions. Answering this question gives you the basis for justifying protective and backup activities for your information processing functions. *Preventive and recovery strategies should be driven first and foremost by business impact.*

4. *Available alternatives.* These are not necessarily tied directly to the nature or extent of the outage as much as the nature of the function and **application** being affected. If certain applications can be carried out manually or with other readily available equipment, then the loss may not be such a big deal. On the other hand, the loss of an 800-number voice network for which there is no viable alternative may spell disaster for a catalog order house. And if the only person who understands the system gets hit by a truck, your alternatives may disappear rapidly.

5. *The cost of recovery and restoration.* In a sense, this a corollary to the nature and extent of the damage.

6. *The time required for recovery and restoration.* The same observation applies. However, in assessing cost and time, remember all those transactions and processes that you were carrying out in a different mode and on different facilities. Getting that backlog caught up on the original or recovered facilities takes much longer than simply returning to your normal mode of processing. Depending on the load you put on your systems and the size of the backlog, it may be impossible to ever get caught up without the use of additional (and usually unplanned for) resources.

Disclosure

Disclosure is a threat that has gotten a lot of coverage in the literature, but to be truthful, I'm not sure that it should rank that high in overall impact or probability. The impact of this threat really depends on the nature of your business. The military and intelligence services (which in many countries, including the United States, have a significant voice in security circles) have given this particular threat a great deal of emphasis, as they should. National or industrial espionage is an important issue. It also makes for great security horror stories and bookshelves full of spy novels.

My message is: Don't blow this one out of proportion. If your industry is prone to industrial espionage or relies heavily on proprietary information, then by all means concentrate on this area. If you are in a position of fiduciary or other form of trust in which confidentiality is key, again, concentrate on this issue.

For certain types of data such as human resources, credit, and medical information, you have an obligation to the data subjects to protect their interests and may be so mandated by law. If you are a defense contractor, the choice has been made for you. But privacy protection, protection against industrial espionage, and related disclosure countermeasures should all be evaluated like other countermeasures. If they apply and have a reasonable level of likelihood and impact, go for it. But don't accept someone else's standards of importance.

Modification

Deliberate modification usually implies some form of fraudulent activity. Accidental modification, on the other hand, is probably the result of poor design or execution.

Let's dispose of a semantic argument that occasionally crops up. Is deliberate and unauthorized *destruction* of data a form of *disruption* or the ultimate form of *modification*? My response is, who cares? In either event, the fundamental question is the same: How do I prevent individuals or processes from performing unauthorized destruction of information resources?

An act of modification may be intended to stop a process or alter the results of a process. In either case, the security specialist needs to know what happened, how it happened, how to prevent a recurrence, how to recover from the current damage, and how to restore the resources. Knowing why it happened may or may not be of interest. It is certainly necessary to the decision-making process if it will change your protective strategy. For example, if the act of modification or destruction was carried out by a disgruntled employee, a new human resources policy may be the appropriate antidote, not more security.

Fraud comes in a variety of flavors. Direct financial fraud is the most common, but consider also the indirect cases. Most prevalent is the claiming of undeserved credentials, such as academic achievement or prior experience or performance, or falsified product tests or quality or performance records. Ultimately, they all come back to some level of financial, social, or status enhancement for the perpetrator.

Protecting against fraud requires a mixture of security and accounting controls. Security addresses the authorization and access control aspects of the process. Are you who you say you are, and are you doing things you're authorized to do? Accounting controls examine whether the authorized processes create appropriate results. Security identifies you as an accounts payable clerk and validates that you are permitted to initiate vendor payments. Accounting controls see to it that you initiate appropriate payments to appropriate individuals.

Here, too, the likelihood of modification is conditioned by the nature of the information, applications, and transactions; the corporate environment; and the people involved. The degree of prevention and detection you impose is also conditioned by the results of a potential defalcation. External requirements such as regulations and laws will also affect your decisions. In fact, legal and regulatory requirements will ease the process of selecting preventive measures. You may have no choice if you wish to comply.

Use

Unauthorized use is probably the most difficult threat to describe because it is so variable. A typical example of unauthorized use of information resources is the second-shift data center supervisor who is running her own real estate business on the company's computers. Theft of service is a good substitute description for this threat.

The reason unauthorized use is difficult to describe with any generality is that unlike the other threat categories, it is highly dependent on corporate policies. For example, some companies encourage the personal use of microprocessors in order to build processing skills. Other organizations regard any departure from strict business usage as a violation. For some types of information resources, it's often impossible to define unauthorized use and hardly worth tracking. The personal use an individual makes of a portable personal computer (PC) is very difficult to determine. You could exert partial control by restricting the types of software that can be loaded on a machine, but even then, can you control whether an employee uses the word-processing facility on his own time to address Christmas cards? Do you really care?

The fundamental issue is the potential harm to the enterprise. The virus is an interesting subject to examine in this context. If, in the process of using a computer for unauthorized activities, someone introduces and uses unauthorized software containing a virus and thus brings down a local area network (LAN), clearly that unauthorized use has produced highly damaging results. If someone uses a PC to design a wedding invitation or a church cake sale announcement on personal time, is it important? Some might argue, with merit, that any unauthorized use is an infraction of the rules and that to permit any infraction is to countenance all infractions. My response is that such an approach is certainly your option. Just be prepared to enforce it fully, fairly, and consistently. Under any circumstances, management owes it to its employees to spell out what it considers authorized and unauthorized usage to be; management must also be ready to enforce the rules it has established.

The Probability Problem

Let's talk a bit about probability. What is the importance of knowing the probability of an occurrence with scientific accuracy? You need enough information to make an appropriate business decision. If you are considering adopting preventive and restorative measures, these should cost no more than the damage they are designed to prevent or restore. Obviously, there is such a thing as too much protection or, at least, spending too much on protection.

Part of the decision-making process in determining how much is enough involves not only the nature, extent, and cost of the damage but also the probability of it occurring at all. The problem is that scientific accuracy is seldom possible, and trying to attain it is seldom worthwhile.

You can narrow the probability problem considerably by breaking threats down into three categories:

1. *Dramatic impact—reasonable probability.* Those events that have enough probability of occurrence and such strong impact that most, if not all, prudent managers would take preventive and recovery steps to deal with them. For example, if your facilities are on an earthquake-prone fault line; if the local power company has a history of blackouts; if your data center is smack in the middle of a flood plain; if the loss of communications could affect your bottom line in twenty-four hours or less; if industrial espionage is common in your industry; if you are more than usually vulnerable to hackers and viruses because of your heavy dependency on communications.

These and similar threats would leave you little alternative but to take contingency measures. How far you go is a function of the value of the resources you're seeking to protect, but at least the expectation of damage is high enough that you don't need to agonize over precise predictions of probability.

2. *Low impact—any probability.* Essentially, this is the so-what category. If it happens, it won't hurt that much and you're not going to waste your time trying to develop probability tables for low-impact events. The trick here is to be sensible in appraising impact. If you feel comfortable that the potential for damage is low, these are the threats you accept, without further analysis.

3. *Significant impact—unknown (but not necessarily unknowable) probability.* These are the areas in which you should concentrate your efforts to establish better estimates of probability. Here you have the greatest likelihood of underspending or overspending in dealing with a specific threat.

Unfortunately, many threats can fit in this category, so try to be pragmatic (see the discussion under the subheading "Prudence or Paranoia?"). Once you've reduced the threats to a manageable number, you have several possible methods available to assess probabilities.

Assessing Probability

For physical threats, there are a number of public and private sources that can provide you with statistics and actuarial estimates of hurricanes, earthquakes, fires, and floods in your area. Public safety organizations, the Army Corps of Engineers, weather and tidal experts, and insurance companies are all good sources. If you have a **risk management** unit in your company, start there.

There is an increasing amount of literature on criminal activity. International, national, state, and local law-enforcement groups are all beginning to gather statistics on computer-related crimes. You may want to start with the National Institute of Justice in Washington, D.C., which provides a comprehensive document and reference service for a nominal fee on a number of areas related to computer crime.

In dealing with disgruntled employees, start closer to home. If you've been around any length of time, you have a feeling for your own organization. For example, if labor relations have been poor in the past, you should certainly pay more attention to the potential for sabotage, modification, or disclosure than you might if employee relations have been exemplary. In this regard, there are trigger events you may wish to take into consideration: layoffs, plant closings or consolidations, attacks on other members of your industry, or being part of a sensitive industry (lately, ecological and animal-rights issues have put otherwise unlikely organizations higher on the vulnerability index).

The nature of your information resources may also lead you to a high vulnerability assessment. If, for example, you rely on widespread public networks, your potential vulnerability could be higher than an essentially closed environment.

Risk Assessment Methodologies

A number of consultants and consulting organizations provide **risk assessment** services. Some use software packages; others depend on personal analysis. Some use both techniques.

Most risk assessment approaches address both impact and probability. They may differ by how the results are presented.

The Qualitative Approach

This approach is often expressed as a descriptive scenario from which tailored judgments and priorities can be developed. Depending on the depth of analysis, you can develop personalized views of each threat as it applies to your organization. It does help you avoid a lot of debate on precise measurements. It can very often be the best way to open up an assessment program, with quantitative measures left for the most critical areas where heavy investment is more likely.

The negatives are several. Depending on the depth of analysis, this approach could cost more, and it usually does not give you a directly quantifiable set of priorities that you can use to measure how much to spend and in what order.

The Quantitative Approach

The two quantitative options—nonmonetarized and monetarized—have the obvious advantage of being more directly responsive to expense-related questions. They also lend themselves to computer-based processes. The downside aspects are several and significant. Most of these approaches are archetypal examples of GIGO (garbage in, garbage out) further aggravated by the belief that anything coming out of a computer must be true. If (and it's a big if) you can provide sufficient, reliable data to these processes, they can provide a pretty reliable index of risk and priority. If not, they may add a patina of pseudoscience and believability to marginally reliable data.

One other observation: The current state of the risk assessment art is more reliable predicting probability and impact of physically related threats such as fire or water damage than logically related events such as hackers or viruses.

The two forms of quantitative risk assessment are:

1. *Nonmonetarized.* This approach usually involves some sort of index or prioritized figure of merit, but may not actually give you a direct dollar figure you can use for return on investment (ROI) analyses.
2. *Monetarized.* Clearly, this approach is the one that is most responsive to your decision-making needs. Unfortunately, it is also the least trustworthy.

Your question, no doubt, is: Which approach do you recommend? My answer is: It depends. Unfortunately, it does. If your organization uses ROI justification, you really don't have much choice. Somewhere in the process, you're going to have to express your recommendations in dollars spent versus dollars at risk. You do, however, have the option of starting with a qualitative approach and converting to a quantitative one after you've developed a more detailed view of your environment. Given little or no constraint on expenses for developing a risk assessment, this is the preferred way, but it is more costly. Some of the more generic quantitative methods can give you good ballpark estimates and even greater precision if your organization looks like the models upon which the methodology is based.

The bottom line is: Which process is best for the decisions you are trying to reach? Define the deliverable you want. Be selective in the method you adopt. Don't be overwhelmed by either computer-based approaches or the personal approach. Even computer-based approaches require interpretation. Talk to others who've been through the process, and don't rush into it.

Prudence or Paranoia?

How far should you go with risk assessment? The quick answer is, only as far as you need to go to get a good perception of the risks you are taking and to justify the expenses you may incur. Some managers, once they embark on risk assessment, develop a mania for more and more precision. Remember, this is not an exact science. The important ingredient to add early in the risk assessment process is the cost and operational implications of the steps you will probably take to deal with those risks. Once you get within range of addressing those expenses, stop. Risk assessment for its own sake may be an interesting exercise, but you're a manager, not a researcher. The objective is to develop an appropriate protection program, not to write a doctoral thesis on the art and science of predicting risk.

Why are you assessing your risk? I'm assuming that you are responsible for information resources that, if compromised or destroyed, could impact your enterprise unfavorably. I used to enjoy a comedian who did a routine with an insurance salesman. He would dig up some of the most outlandish situations under which his potential insurer would have to pay off, such as, "Suppose a nearsighted male polar bear escapes from the zoo and mistakes my white Volkswagen for a female polar bear. If, in the course of its amorous advances, my car is destroyed, will you pay off?" The moral of the story is, keep introducing reality checks into your risk assessment process. If your enterprise is typical, you don't have to exercise much imagination to develop a set of real risks.

The second point to remember is that information protection is a process, not an event. If you don't catch everything the first time, don't worry. You have probably made the right decisions for the risks you have addressed, and very few protection budgets allow you to broadside the whole enterprise. Plan to review your risks on a regular, periodic basis or whenever a trigger event takes place, such as new technology, new applications, new organization, a security or continuity incident, or new regulatory requirements.

Don't get caught up in the all-or-nothing frame of mind. You may hear: "Either we have a complete protection system or it's not worth doing." Nonsense! Incremental protective measures are usually the only sensible way to embark on a program. Complete protection is an illusion, and an undesirable illusion at that. If you want your information resources to be totally protected, shut them down. The minute you begin using them, they are exposed to some level of risk. So are you when you cross a street, ride a bus or airplane, drive a car, or speak to a stranger. You are trying to minimize the most likely risks, not eliminate all risks. Be careful what you promise your management. You may be held to it—to your and management's disadvantage.

5

Who's Involved in Information Protection?

What's in this chapter?
- The Identity and Role of the Owner
- The Identity and Role of the User
- The Identity and Role of the Service Supplier
- Management Responsibilities
- The Specialists
  —Data Security Administration
  —Continuity Administration
  —MIS and Network Management
  —Data and Database Management
  —Applications Developers
  —Internal Audit
  —Convergence of Security and Continuity
- The Solo Manager

If one reality pervades today's **information** processing world, it is interdependency. **Information protection** (IP), if it is to be effective, has to recognize that reality. An effective IP strategy must ensure that all the players in an information **system** not only protect themselves but also contribute to the protection of others. The term *system* itself implies mutuality of responsibility. On the road, driving defensively is not enough. We have to drive with a consciousness that other lives depend on us. There is a strong parallel in information processing.

In this age of networked systems and software/data interchange, the issue of mutual responsibility is not only real, it is pressing. Yesterday's view that "self-protection equals total protection" is not only dead, it's deadly—a concept to be kept in mind as we begin our discussion of responsibilities.

42

For the rest of this chapter, I discuss different classes of information protection responsibility. Please keep one important point uppermost in mind throughout the following discussion: Each class describes a set of responsibilities and roles; in any organization, one person can fulfill several roles, and several people can share the same role. The ratio is seldom one-to-one.

The Identity and Role of the Owner

Let's dispel a common misconception about the term *ownership* as it's used in the information protection literature. I am not talking about the IP equivalent of a title search. If there is any dispute about more than one organization or individual having the copyright or "rights-in-data" associated with a specific file or database, those discussions are best left to the lawyers. I am talking about something far more pragmatic and, in a sense, more arbitrary. For our purposes, the information owner is the individual who determines the following for a specific file, **application**, database, or **information resource:**

- Who can use it?
- What can users do—read, write, update?
- The circumstances under which they can do it—during prime shift, only through preauthorized software and devices?
- The conditions for use—written approval, belonging to a specific department, simply being an employee in good standing, a member of an inter-enterprise consortium?

Being assigned ownership may have absolutely nothing to do with the normal modes of acquiring ownership, such as investment or original development responsibility. These factors may have a bearing, but they're not necessary. What we are looking for is operational responsibility for the use of the resource. Most frequently, this is assigned to a manager. However, senior professionals can also carry out this function. But whoever it is should be someone who is in the best position to make intelligent and timely decisions about the use of the information resource and can carry the burden of responsibility for its misuse.

Ultimately, as for everything else in the enterprise, top management is responsible, but there are specific authorization, accountability, and audit processes associated with IP that are best handled at a lower organizational level. The surrogate who acts on top management's behalf and determines and ensures implementation of the protective strategy for an information resource is the owner. As a line manager in an information-dependent environment, *you* may well be that person. But before you can carry out these responsibilities, several things have to take place:

- Some risk analysis about the data resource, no matter how informal
- Establishment of a classification of the resource and identification of appropriate protective measures
- A completed determination of where, when, how, and by whom the resource will be used
- Assignment of ownership responsibility and its acknowledgment by all concerned parties
- Existence of enforcement and compliance measurement mechanisms

If all that sounds dreadfully bureaucratic, it needn't be. If you think about how you assign responsibility for any task in your management sphere, it's no different. You may normally use techniques that are more informal, intuitive, and even unstated, but the process is there. In the case of IP, it helps to be more formal about the process, because as I've said, information protection doesn't come naturally.

The Identity and Role of the User

Notice that I don't use the term *end user*. I'd like to get rid of that term, but it's an uphill semantic battle. *End* implies a passive sort of relationship established through a dumb terminal and predetermined by the processing logic of an almighty mainframe. It was that way once, but no longer. Today's user often has more horsepower and processing options than the owner.

The user is an individual or process that interacts with the information resource. The inclusion of the word *process* is important. Although it's almost always possible to trace a processing activity back to a specific person or persons for whose benefit the work is being done, there may be any number of processes that occur in between.

The purpose of establishing user identity is to enable the protection of the information resource by controlling access and process options on the owner's behalf. To do that, you must be able to catalog all of the users—both individuals and processes—so that you can then establish what their rights should be. *These are business decisions, not technical decisions.* You may use technology to enforce your decisions, but the access rules for users should be set according to business criteria. What do they need to be able to do their jobs? Does that need compromise **security** or availability in some way? If not, fine. If so, what has priority, business need or protection? That is a management decision and should be based on business risk criteria.

It is up to the users to comply with the rules set down by the owner and implemented by the information protection infrastructure, such as security administrators, access control software, or key cards for physical access. To do that, they must cooperate with the protective process.

Take password management as an example. If your access control system calls for nontrivial passwords of a specific length and content (e.g., nonrepetitive alphanumerics) that in turn must be kept confidential and changed as required, the users are responsible for doing so. If password sharing is forbidden, users must not share passwords. And if users see violations in the making, they should report them— not easy to do or to enforce, but necessary for good information protection.

On the other hand, if users believe they are being hampered by overly strict or cumbersome protective measures, they must have an avenue to seek change and improvement. The protection system exists for the enterprise, not the other way around. If you are losing productivity because the reins are too tight, then the reins need to be loosened. Users should be encouraged to make their case.

With a little reflection, it's clear that the same individual can be both owner and user—even of the same information resources. They must behave differently under each circumstance, and it's management's responsibility to ensure that they understand what is required in each case.

The Identity and Role of the Service Supplier

When first introduced, the term *service supplier* usually evokes images of a large information service bureau, network, or turnkey operator such as GEISCO, EDS, or ADP. These service suppliers belong in this category, but at one extreme. At the other extreme is the individual—a secretary or clerk—who maintains manual files. In between are all sorts of folks such as local area network (LAN) administrators, management information systems (MIS), and database and network managers and their staffs.

The distinguishing characteristic of service suppliers is that they act as intermediaries between the owner and the user in supplying the services required for useful information processing to take place. Often, they do not have firsthand knowledge of the applications in which the owner and user are involved. They are involved in supplying the appropriate technological and administrative **platforms** for the application.

The role of service suppliers in IP is to provide the technical and administrative vehicles required to fulfill the protection requirements laid down by the owner. It is their responsibility to maintain the inherent integrity and effectiveness of the protective system. Although the requirements come from the owner, and may be interpreted by the security specialists, it is the suppliers who are the providers.

Suppliers may also be owners and users. Consider all of the system platform-related software and hardware they use in order to make processing power available to users and their applications. The platform is in a real sense owned and used by the supplier, who must fulfill all three roles. Does this create a conflict? It can. Ask your internal auditors for their opinions. By the nature of their functions, suppliers are usually granted rather extraordinary privileges when it comes to security. Often those privileges are much wider than they need to be to fulfill business needs.

Another term advanced by many IP specialists is *custodian.* I've stopped using it in order to avoid confusion. Half the people I know who use the term treat it as a synonym for *owner;* the other half equate it with *service supplier.* You can probably see the logic for either interpretation. I prefer to avoid the term altogether, but if your organization uses it, make sure you all agree on its meaning.

Management Responsibilities

In addition to the explicit and implicit management responsibilities contained in the roles I've already discussed, there are four other management functions that are key to developing and maintaining a cost-effective, consistent, comprehensive, and appropriate information protection program.

1. *Motivation.* Unless management—top, middle, and first-line—demonstrates and communicates its interest and dedication to an effective IP program, nothing worthwhile will happen. This takes more than a letter posted on a bulletin board. It involves personal example and persistent emphasis. You don't get results in this area with an occasional mention. You may be getting tired of hearing it, but I will repeat that you are dealing with a process that doesn't come naturally and needs extraordinary motivation.

2. *Facilitation.* Management cannot expect a successful program if it demonstrates an unwillingness to modify behavior; originate or alter policies, standards, procedures, and guidelines; provide money and resources; and support appropriate decisions.

3. *Organization.* If management buries the IP function and process, then it shouldn't be surprised if they act dead. There are many flexible organizational options available to suit different corporate or institutional cultures and structures. Most important is to put protection administration under the authority of people who have the skills, resources, and motivation to make it work. Classical organizational chart symmetry or purity should be secondary.

4. *Prioritization.* All levels of management need to give their own personal attention to the process, actively and passively. Keeping your door open to IP issues is better than having it closed. Going out the door and demonstrating an active interest in the ongoing state and process of protection is infinitely superior.

The Specialists

So far I've been talking about the information protection roles of individuals involved in generic information processing and usage. They are the front line in any effective program. If it's not working there, it's not working anywhere.

Let's turn now to those individuals with special roles to play in this process. Depending on the size and nature of your enterprise, you may have all, some, or possibly none of them. In many companies, the same individual may carry out several of these roles.

Data Security Administration

There are several major data security (DS) functions, and they may be found at different levels of the organization. In most large enterprises, there is a corporate or headquarters DS function and similar functions in divisions and departments that are heavy users of information resources, especially critical information resources.

I have switched terms from information protection to data security and **continuity** because most organizations still separate the security and continuity functions, sometimes in widely diverse parts of their operations. (A little later in this chapter, I make the case for converging the two.) For the moment, I focus on the security function— prevention of unauthorized disruption, disclosure, modification, and use.

I use the term DS *function* instead of *administrator* because the number or fraction of individuals assigned at each level is load-dependent. *Warning: Making DS administration a small part of a lot of people's job descriptions is a surefire formula for failure. You need a focal point and a motivated critical mass; small increments of overworked people's time do not get DS programs off the deck.*

Members of a DS Administration (DSA) function administer the processes of authorization, identification, verification, access control, accountability, and security audit (see Chapter 9 for more details).

Under an access control system, each individual, process, and resource should be both uniquely identified and assigned and described through authorization characteristics or "rules." Who or what are you? What can you do or (if you're a resource) have done to you? The identification and authorization process is often administered by the DSA function—if not directly under its control, then usually subject to its oversight.

The DSA also helps to develop, and is often the keeper of, data security policies, standards, and procedures. As usual, position on the organizational chart dictates the scope of this responsibility. A corporate DSA function will generally have responsibility for the corporate office and often for the entire enterprise. Division and department functions should, but don't always, have an appropriately scaled down responsibility. There is no single appropriate structure. The ideal way is the one that best fits your culture and organization.

In addition, the DSA function often has responsibilities related to the physical security of information resources and physical access to processing areas such as data centers, network control centers, and media libraries.

Data security may also be the means by which security violations are reported to line management. There's an important concept here: To be successful, a security program requires that user management be directly involved at a number of points—authorization, awareness, motivation, and adjudication of violations. The DSA function, operations, or sometimes internal audit may supply the evidence, but it's the user's management that carries the responsibility for handling the issue. Don't try to pass it off to a staff function, and whatever you do, don't ignore it.

Security assessment or audit is often the subject of the greatest organizational debate. The debate is usually between the DSA function and the EDP specialists in internal audit, and it usually focuses on the question of objectivity. If the DSA function is part of MIS, can it be objective in its judgments about security? The point is valid but, in my opinion, overdone.

There is a significant case to be made for having both groups assess the security characteristics of the organization's information resources. The most compelling reason is that even with both groups putting combined effort into an assessment program, there are usually insufficient people to meet the workload. That's why they often turn to outside consultants and external audit.

In those cases in which objectivity is a significant issue, internal audit should have first call. But in most areas, assessment by the DS function or even self-audit by the business function itself is better than no coverage. I believe strongly in self-assessment and peer assessment as pragmatic and effective techniques for extending the ways in which an enterprise can examine its security (and continuity) status.

However, the internal and external auditors' views of their scopes of responsibility are often different from that of the DS Administrator. The audit function often, and appropriately, regards its primary job as reporting on the current state of security, not on directing how problems should be solved.

Finally, the DSA function is often the primary developer of security education and awareness programs. I am a firm believer in strong line-management participation in these programs, but support by trained specialists in development, administration, execution, and evaluation will greatly enhance the end result.

Should your enterprise have a DSA function? Yes! Should your enterprise have a *separate and distinct* DSA organization? It depends on the degree of perceived risk and vulnerability, potential workload, the nature and scope of the information resources you have, and available budget and resources.

Please avoid this common mistake: Don't judge the need for a separate DSA function on the basis of the size and type of hardware you have installed. A very strong case can be made that an enterprise with a large number of distributed intermediate and microprocessors has a greater need for a full-time DSA function than a data center full of heavy iron.

LANs seldom get the depth of management they deserve. They almost never get the level of security they require. Because they usually grow from the bottom up, management is often ad hoc. If you look at the applications and information resources currently being supported by LANs in your organization and compare them to the mainframe load, you may come away disturbed. If you examine future trends, you'll probably become even more disturbed. In most companies, the workload on LANs has subtly but steadily increased in both magnitude and importance. LAN management hasn't kept pace.

Continuity Administration

A term often used for continuity is *availability*. Frequently, you'll also hear the terms *contingency planning, disaster recovery,* and *business resumption.* These last three all tend to concentrate on after-the-fact recovery as opposed to prevention *and* recovery.

The trend in continuity planning and development is to balance prevention with recovery. In many cases, where an effective backup scenario is impractical or impossible, the trend is to concentrate almost exclusively on prevention. Instead of picking yourself up after you've fallen, the emphasis has shifted to not falling in the first place, or at least vastly reducing the odds of falling.

The two main responsibilities of the continuity administration function are as follows:

1. *The development* and maintenance *of appropriate, comprehensive, consistent, and cost-effective business recovery plans.* Business **recovery** plans (see Chapter 10 for more details), as the name suggests, involve a great deal more than computer backup. Indeed, the computer may be a secondary concern. People, communications, and other resources may overshadow the hardware.

2. *The business recovery plan test function.* At an information protection conference, I asked an audience of several hundred people, "How many of your organizations have a disaster (contingency, business recovery) plan?" Most of the audience raised their hands. Next question: "How many of your organizations have a *tested* disaster

(contingency, business recovery) plan? About 20 percent replied affirmatively. The next question got almost no positive replies: "How many of your organizations have a *successfully tested* plan?" Fundamental as it may seem, there are very few fully tested plans that are really known to be appropriate and to work. There are many reasons why organizations are reluctant to fully test their plans: prior knowledge that the plan won't survive a test, cost, lack of resources or time, fear of disruption caused by the test, fear of failure. If you don't have a tested and validated plan, you don't have a plan.

Similar to information security, a continuity awareness program is key to a successful continuity program. Although backup and recovery are a little more obvious and less unnatural than information security, most people leave it until the rest of the chores are cleared away—which is never. An increasing number of organizations mandate file backup, especially for personal computers (PCs), but how and what to back up and the steps to efficient, secure backup are often left out of the discussion. In today's world of viruses, misdirected backup procedures can actually promote the spread of viruses.

Preventive strategies and measures are an important part of any continuity program. As I mentioned earlier, being able to recover from an outage is often not enough. Increasingly, the requirement is to avoid outages in the first place. This puts the continuity administrator in a different position with different priorities.

MIS and Network Management

Obviously, security and continuity administrators do not provide results by themselves. What about MIS and network management? Are they involved? You bet! In fact, in some organizations, the security and continuity function may report to MIS (or less frequently to network) management.

The primary responsibility of MIS and network managers is to provide the appropriate hardware and software platforms and operating environments to support the information protection strategies, policies, procedures, and mechanisms selected and developed by management and the protection specialists. They should also provide expertise in determining which technical mechanisms, such as access control software or encryption devices, are appropriate. The MIS and network managers in many organizations may be the same person or at least belong to the same department. Network management, especially, is a new and incomplete art, and security management for networks is still in its adolescence.

Data and Database Management

If an organization is going to take a formal, structured approach to protecting its information resources, it must be able to identify those resources as well as the processes and individuals that use them. Data administration, which sets the general rules for data identification and usage, and database administration, which carries out those rules using many different tools and techniques, are often the only functions within an organization that have a truly comprehensive (and accurate) view of its information resources.

For example, consistent and meaningful naming conventions for information resources are an important structure upon which to classify data, users, and processes. Without such conventions, ambiguity and mismanagement can rapidly creep into the information system. If you can't accurately identify what you're supposed to protect, there's a good chance of missing the target.

Applications Developers

Security comes in a variety of forms. Controlling access to applications is a major function. How an application controls access to itself and the other resources it uses is key. Today, many applications developers rely on generic, operating system–related access control subsystems. These subsystems, such as IBM's RACF (Resource Access Control Facility) or Computer Associates' ACF2 or Top Secret, work in concert with the operating system and other subsystems and applications to form a comprehensive protection system.

Some developers still provide their own access control functions, as either a supplement to or a substitute for the generic subsystems. Their reasons may or may not be particularly valid. The problems with using these individual processes are related to update, maintenance, and consistency.

There are two other important ways in which applications developers get involved in information protection:

1. *Management of change.* What means do the developers use to ensure that application updates are properly designed, implemented, tested, and deployed? Can someone alter the application process in

such a way as to permit unauthorized modification, disclosure, or destruction of data? Who controls the developers? Are they and/or the systems programmers who maintain the operating system given carte blanche privileges? They should at least operate in a well-audited environment.

2. *Ruggedness or robustness of the application design and implementation.* This is a continuity concern. Not all systems and applications interruptions result from physical failures. Increasingly, logically induced failures account for more and more losses.

Overly complex, poorly designed, poorly maintained, and inadequately tested programs (and poorly designed networks) can cause as much grief as a leak or a fire. A positive security and continuity side effect from the use of Computer-Aided Software Engineering (CASE) techniques for program development is the imposition of a discipline and consistency on the programming process, which can result in more stable code.

Internal Audit

The role of internal audit in information protection may vary dramatically from enterprise to enterprise. Specifically, this section looks at the role of EDP audit within internal audit.

EDP auditors frequently carry the responsibility for assessing the effectiveness of controls, security, and continuity in the company's systems and applications, including procedures and administration. However, resources and skills constraints coupled with extreme workloads can erode their effectiveness. As a manager, you ought to develop an informed opinion about how—and how effectively—internal audit operates in reviewing security and continuity, especially for systems and applications that may not be included in the company's financial system and therefore may not be covered as part of the financial audit process. Ask similar questions about your external auditors.

Convergence of Security and Continuity

Continuity should be a joint responsibility of the DS function and the continuity administrator. Why? For certain classes of outages, especially the nonphysical (or so-called logical) outage, the issue involves both. Take the virus as an example. The security issues are plain: How did it get in here? Where is it, and how many of them are there? How do we get rid of them? The continuity issues are equally plain: How do we repair the damage and recover operations in such a way that we catch up, don't lose any control, and don't induce reinfection? Both groups are involved in minimizing impact.

Too many enterprises separate security and continuity functionally and organizationally. Often continuity is the responsibility of someone within operations, while security may be a separate group, person, or part-person in any number of different departments. I am not arguing for organizational mergers as much as greater cooperation and joint planning and budgeting. The problems are converging; so should the problem-handling mechanisms.

The Solo Manager

As I went through this litany of all the potential departmental and functional players who could be involved in security and continuity, I'm sure some of you were saying: "Hey, that may be great for huge money-center banks, retail chains, and governmental agencies, but I'm all there is—me and my LAN or IBM AS/400, DEC/VAX, or microprocessor. If I had all those departments, I probably wouldn't be reading this book." If that's your situation, what do *you* do?

If you have to perform all the functions I mentioned above by yourself, they're probably not going to get done. Don't despair or quit; there's hope. In the first place, the odds are good that you have a relatively small number of critical applications and information resources to really worry about. (Yes, I know there are exceptions.) The first thing you should do is get a practical handle on what those resources are and how critical they are to your organization. Whether you're one autonomous department in a large but highly decentralized company, a small business function like a doctor's office or a health maintenance organization (HMO), a public or semipublic entity like a village or county office, or a museum or a charitable organization, there are a limited number of key applications and information files that you cannot afford to lose, become unavailable, be disclosed, or be fraudulently altered.

Start out by trusting your knowledge of your corner of the business and get advice from other managers whose judgment you trust. Use only those forms and mechanisms that will help you formalize that view. That could be one of the **risk assessment** packages on the market, which vary in price from several hundreds to tens of thousands of dollars. Obviously, the cost of the risk assessment package should not exceed the estimated cost of the potential damage you're trying to assess and avoid.

You might be able to do the whole thing on a spreadsheet or simple database and, in certain circumstances, with pencil and paper. I've provided an example in Figure 5-1, but you can make your own just as easily.

Try your best to note not only the information files but the applications that run against those resources and who the owners and users are. There is one characteristic that may make simple application-by-application notation a bit misleading. That's interdependence: Application X depends on Application Y for its input, and this in turn provides data to Application Z. Obviously, if Application X fails, the whole daisy chain could collapse. But once again, remember that you are trying to get your arms around the universe of the information resources you want to protect.

Once you have a view of the resources, their value, and some thoughts on potential risk, review the bidding. If the number and variety of resources look big, relative to your organization, further analysis of risk and prioritization of targets may be warranted to optimize your protective investment. If not, you can start with some basics.

First basic question: What's the bigger issue—security or continuity? Are you concerned about unavailability, or data getting into the wrong hands? Are viruses driving you up the wall? Is fraud the issue, or vandalism, or leakage to the press or competitors? Notice that these are all business questions, and you may not want to answer them by yourself. Get other opinions before making a decision. Don't start making major investments until you do.

Once you've got a reasonably good picture of where to prioritize, you can begin to explore options such as investing in antiviral software, a LAN manager with good security features, a hard disk access control package, or a tape device for backup and recovery.

Deciding whether and how you will protect a device such as a microprocessor or LAN file server should be a *result* of the risk analysis—not the other way around. It's tempting to take short-cuts. Many organizations take the approach that if they protect the computer, the information is protected. But it doesn't always work that way, because you need to protect information and the processes that affect and use it. Information doesn't stay in one place. How do you treat it after you extract it for reports or queries? You probably

Figure 5–1.   Risk assessment form.

CRITICAL INFORMATION RESOURCE ANALYSIS		
Business Function:		
Resource Name: (File Name, Processor, Network, Environment)		
Owner:		
Application 1:	**Users:**	**Classifications:** Confidentiality
	Environment:	Integrity
		Availability
Application 2:	**Users:**	**Classifications:** Confidentiality
	Environment:	Integrity
		Availability
Application 3:	**Users:**	**Classifications:** Confidentiality
	Environment:	Integrity
		Availability
Application 4:	**Users:**	**Classifications:** Confidentiality
	Environment:	Integrity
		Availability
Application 5:	**Users:**	**Classifications:** Confidentiality
	Environment:	Integrity
		Availability
Application 6:	**Users:**	**Classifications:** Confidentiality
	Environment:	Integrity
		Availability
Major threats:		**Highest Classifications:** Confidentiality
		Integrity
		Availability
Comments:		

This, or a similar form, can be used to develop a prioritized list of information resources needing protection. Describe the resource by name and type, indicate the owner by name or department, and the applications that use the resource. For each usage, indicate a level of confidentiality, integrity, and availability required. Also note the authorized users and the processing environment employed by the users, e.g. mainframe, PC, Lan etc.

do more than one thing to that information. How do you control those processes? Who can perform them? What can they do, and under what circumstances? You may send the information elsewhere. What controls are in effect over that transmission? See what I mean?

The information must be the focal point of your protective efforts. What you do to protect hardware and processing software should be driven by your information protection strategy, not the other way around. Keeping that simple point in mind will help to ensure that your investments of time, effort, and dollars bear maximum fruit.

Most security and continuity programs are made up of about 70 percent administration and procedure and 30 percent technology. So before you start purchasing and installing protective devices and software, you should write down some basic guidelines and procedures you want to follow. Keep them simple for starters; you can always add flourishes later. Determine who will authorize usage. How will usage be authorized (written, verbal, countersigned)? Who will be authorized? What will they be authorized to do? You can usually state these in terms of types of access to individual resources: read only (see but don't touch), originate, update, destroy. Yes, destroy. Oddly enough, many security programs as originally written are so oriented toward protection that they make no provision for getting rid of obsolete or incorrect data.

Before you start developing from scratch, check to see what's already around. You may find procedures, guidelines, standards, and policies that already exist in your organization. You'd be surprised (or maybe you wouldn't) by how much material on this subject resulting from a task force or earlier effort at security is gathering dust in fancy binders in some credenza or file. If anyone in your organization knows whether these materials exist and where they are, the internal auditor or general security officer should know. They may be the only ones who are using them. (This, of course, assumes your organization has either of these functions.)

Of course, the material you find may not be helpful. It may even be counterproductive because it may not reflect the current patterns of information processing and usage in your organization. Most information protection programs began life with a strong mainframe orientation because that's where most of the information was processed. Times have obviously changed, but unfortunately, security policies and guidelines are slower in keeping up. But if you never had a mainframe, it's less likely you'll have this problem.

Some organizations, in an effort to satisfy a legal, regulatory, or audit requirement with minimum effort or pain, will borrow, with little or no adaptation, some other organization's security and continuity policies, standards, or guidelines. When I worked for IBM, we made our program available publicly because so many enterprises asked for it as a model. I always wondered how a company with over 300,000 employees, operating in close to 150 nations, and utilizing more computing power than most countries (and displaying near paranoia about information protection) could be a useful model for so many other enterprises. I have also seen major sections of IBM's and other companies' security and continuity policies and standards lifted wholesale into some organizations' manuals. You get to recognize the terminology and style.

Nevertheless, knowing what exists in your company policy and standards manuals will probably give you some perspective on what has gone on, the degree to which standards and policies are used, and the degree to which, at least formally, you can write your own ticket. Of course, even if policies and standards do exist, if they are honored primarily in the breach, you probably still have a great deal of freedom. Once again, if you don't have any of this stuff to look at, you also don't have to worry about running afoul of it.

You're now at the point of actually putting into place some administrative and technological safeguards. There are just two points I want to make before ending this chapter. They apply to everyone and all circumstances, but they are especially important if you are a one-person show:

1. Do not allow yourself to get bulldozed into committing more than you can deliver. Information protection programs often come into being as a result of crises or mandates from on high. Both usually have an overblown sense of urgency attached to them. This may sound peculiar coming from an information protection advocate, but urgency can often be your worst enemy. It can often result in poorly thought-out and poorly executed programs. Give yourself time, realistic goals, and room to make a few mistakes. Don't doom yourself to failure before you start.

2. Even more important, realize that there is no such thing as total security. Thank God! If there were, its effect on the organization would be so debilitating that the company would soon cease to function. An important corollary to that is: Partial programs will have a

beneficial effect. Just because you can't afford a state-of-the-art burglar alarm system in your home doesn't mean you shouldn't lock the doors and windows. The same principle applies.

Build your program in increments and measure the increments in terms of additional security and continuity gained, not how far you are from perfection. By all means, continue to upgrade your program. (Your auditors probably won't give you any choice.) But also make sure that your management understands the incremental value of the measures you've installed. Make sure you create the appropriate expectations on the part of your management. If not, it will haunt you.

Developing and Maintaining an Information Protection Program

6

Getting Support for Your Information Protection Program

The first step in proposing and justifying an **information protection** (IP) program is to develop a clear concept of what you want to do and why you want to do it. It sounds absurdly simple, but it's not—especially the *why* part. You may have more guidance and suggestions on what to do than you really need, but determining why can be more elusive.

Proposing an IP Program

The initial impetus for the creation of an IP program can come from different sources:

- *Management may request it.* You may be motivated to get a program off the deck by a one-line message from the front office:

"Make our computers (network, **information,** data) secure by (usually an absurdly short date)." This could be the result of an audit comment or an incident, and the temptation is great to do something (anything) to show that you're a conscientious, right-thinking, responsive, up-and-coming manager. There's no question that being "unresponsive" can be a career-limiting move. However, the first lesson in proposing an IP program, even if requested from on high, is that top management reserves the right to be inconsistent, especially when faced with the prospect of spending money, allocating resources, restricting freedom, or stepping on political or cultural toes. "You asked for it" doesn't qualify as a statement of justification, especially if top management cannot or chooses not to remember the request. A request (command) from the executive suite or an equivalent source, such as the audit committee, may be a motivator, but it is not in itself sufficient justification for an IP program.

• *You may decide that you need an IP program.* You have come to the realization (no doubt persuaded by this text) that your valuable **information resources** are insufficiently protected, and you want to do something about it. Your perception of management's attitude is that it is (1) noncomittal, (2) hostile, (3) unknown, or (4) all of the above. I'm not suggesting that your management is schizophrenic; I'm suggesting that there's more than one of them.

Once you've decided (for whatever reason) that you need an IP program, what should you propose? Start with those areas that are going to produce noticeable, short-range results and will make a significant contribution to management's overall objectives. You may not be able to take on the most pressing problems immediately for good and sufficient reasons: lack of infrastructure, complexity of the problem, insufficient experience, or insufficient resources. Show the more complex and difficult issues as future development (with specific dates, if necessary).

Obviously, if you have a near and present danger such as a rash of virus attacks, you don't have much choice. But if you are developing an IP program without any immediate specific pressure, take advantage of the situation and propose activities that have high visibility, high chance of success, and can produce high returns on relatively low investments.

An Awareness Program

One such highly visible activity—an awareness program—is a good bet for a couple of reasons:

1. No matter how technical the environment, people will make or break your **security** program. They should be your first target.
2. An awareness program is nontechnical. Senior management can understand what you're doing. Remember, you're in a start-up mode, and early visibility, "buy-in," and success are important.

Starting immediately with technical activities such as installing an access control system may be tempting. You'd be aiming at the heart of the problem—protecting computer-based information. Unfortunately, you need a procedural infrastructure to get any real use out of the access control technology—some form of classification system, authorization procedures, password administration, and rules writing, no matter how rudimentary. In order to get that infrastructure off the ground (even in a small department), you need user cooperation and participation. An awareness program, if done right, can do that for you (see Chapter 15 for details on awareness program content).

There is another subtle but important element that results from kicking off an awareness program first. You have to tell your audience what you want them to do. Therefore, you need some statements of company policy and procedure for security and **continuity** (again, no matter how rudimentary). If you proposed a policy-writing exercise directly, you might get tied up in a major bureaucratic venture, or the whole program might be put on the back burner. The awareness program gives you a tangible reason, here and now, for developing employee guidance (a substitute term for policies and procedures, if they are not popular in your enterprise).

There are a number of awareness programs available from vendors, complete with films, handouts, posters, guidebooks, and other useful materials. Many consultants and consulting firms, including my employer, can produce an awareness program for you. Many organizations will provide you with some of their materials free of charge. There's lots of material available and you'd be foolish not to take advantage of it. However, under no circumstances should you launch any form of ready-made program without making significant custom alterations to it. Include strong company identification and fit it to your organization, environment, culture, and objectives. Unless your audience recognizes the program as a *company* or department program (not just a company-sponsored program) that has a strong and pervasive element of unique company proprietorship, they are going to put it into the same category as generic public-service communications on social, health, medical, or other issues. They'll look at it as something the company is doing out of good corporate citizenship, not something that directly affects company operations. Take the additional time to make the program your own. It will be worth it.

Getting Management's Support

Which of the following mission statements for an information protection program would sell better in your organization?

1. To prevent serious loss or compromise of the enterprise's critical information resources.
2. To provide a secure and stable information processing platform for the continued growth and profitability of the enterprise.

They are both valid statements and, depending on the mind-set of the approving management, either can be effective. Given a choice, however, I'll take the second one every time. It's positive; it aligns information protection with the objectives of information processing, which in turn are aligned with the objectives of the enterprise. It speaks to what motivates top management, and it puts you in the position of being a contributor to, rather than an inhibitor of, growth.

Occasionally, when I've made this recommendation to security professionals, technicians, and other managers, I've been accused of being transparently cute and playing semantic games. In self-defense, I believe that the most essential characteristic of a successful security officer or a manager proposing a protection program is the ability to speak convincingly to business management in terms that it understands and believes. Technical competence is a necessary but insufficient condition for success. Business people listen to business people.

In practical terms, what does this mean? Should we scrap **risk assessment** and the prioritization of threats and protective measures

I talked about in the earlier chapters? Of course not. They are the essentials of your program. But let's examine two different approaches to the same circumstance.

USGUYS is in the parts distribution business. A number of its major customers want to have access to its catalog in electronic form. Because of the volatility of the parts market—both prices and specifications—as well as the desire to do on-line ordering, it makes sense to consider a dial-up catalog facility instead of sending out diskettes or some other form of electronic update. USGUYS is going to allow outsiders to have direct access to its system and data.

Are there potential security issues? You bet! How to approach them? The USGUYS IP manager has two options:

1. Deluge the responsible management with a catalog of all the possible foul-ups, threats, and embarrassments that could occur in order to bridle its cockeyed optimism and get it to work on a security program.
2. Sit down with management and project how much more effective a stable, error-free, well-controlled system would be for customer satisfaction, future expansion, and increased volume and profitability.

It might be a tough sell either way, because security could impact cost, overhead, performance, schedules, and resources. But at least the second approach sells benefits. Unfortunately for the first alternative, most business managers don't categorize avoiding threats as a benefit. They regard it as a nonevent—a bad thing that didn't happen.

The key to getting support for your IP program is to make it a positive contributor in management's eyes. It sounds obvious, but if you could read some of the security program proposals I've seen, you'd know that the obvious doesn't always get done. Don't claim the impossible or try to sweep costs under the rug, but do present the program in the best possible light.

Another helpful strategy is to find a powerful ally. If you can find a supportive member of operating management, especially someone who is highly dependent on your information and is also contributing directly to the organization's bottom line, that person can be extremely valuable in getting a program off the ground. Here's an example.

When I worked for IBM as Corporate Director of Information Security Programs, my major orientation was toward IBM's customers, our product line and market support, and our external relations with governments, the public, and the press. I had a tangential interest in and relationship to IBM's own protection programs, since IBM used a great deal of its own products and, in a sense, was another large customer I had to worry about. Nevertheless, the IBM internal security program belonged to a different directorate. At one point, our internal security was rolling along adequately, but my colleagues were somewhat anxious to install further technological and administrative improvements. They weren't making a lot of progress.

[*This situation, by the way, is often more difficult to deal with than start-up. The justification for incremental security improvements runs up against the "What's wrong with what we've got?" syndrome. Here you have the double bind of trying to justify additional resources and activities without impugning the effectiveness of what you've already done. Once again, make sure management understands what you plan to do and what you're leaving undone.*]

Back at IBM, all the pressure and persuasion by the corporate staff functions weren't bearing a great deal of fruit. Then, one day, the president of one of IBM's major development divisions was presented with an extremely accurate description of one of our new and unannounced technologies. Unfortunately, the description was on the front page of a widely read industry journal.

Needless to say, he hit the roof and cited quite accurately and vehemently the lost competitive advantage and marketing flexibility that resulted from the article. Unauthorized disclosure of information had hit his operation at the bottom line. Actually, it was the result of a different type of information security problem—a couple of voluble engineers talking out of school had created the problem, not any direct failure of the information processing security program. But the side effects were significant. Information protection was tightened on all fronts and my staff colleagues got their program blessed and more.

I'm not advocating that you go out and create incidents for the sake of motivating management, but do take the time and effort to try to establish alliances with the high-level line managers who have the most to lose. If you get their support, it can be incredibly valuable. If you can't get their support, at least try to neutralize them. In the final analysis, management with direct bottom-line responsibility swings more weight than staff management. Don't cut out the concerned staffs, but don't stop with them. And if you, yourself, are a line manager with bottom-line influence, use that position for all it's worth.

Once you have the support, get the program established. Get out of the special-handling mode and into business as usual as rapidly as you can. The best way to do this is to keep the initial program horizon relatively short range. But make sure your management knows it's short range. Tell senior management "This is what we need to get started, and here's what we'll get out of it. You are making an investment that has both a short- and a long-range return." This understanding is imperative. If management thinks your requirements are one-time only and it will never be hearing from you again, you have created an inextricable dilemma for yourself.

Information protection is a process, not an event. You might want to repeat that periodically in front of your mirror and your management. Don't be apologetic about it. Just about everything else in your business is process driven. Even major capital investments require maintenance. Why should information protection, which is supporting the ongoing information process, which is, in turn, supporting the ongoing business process, be anything but ongoing itself?

Getting Support From Your Peers

Senior management's "buy-in" is only the first step. The fact that senior management wants a protection program will, at best, get you a hearing among your management peers. It may also get you sympathy. It will not necessarily get you cooperation and support.

I make presentations at quite a few information protection seminars each year. Many of them are for IP specialists. One of the most popular topics at these events is how to get top management's support. The fact that security specialists are concerned with management support is a good sign. What's disturbing is the rather naive assumption that top management's approval will open all doors and smooth all roads. It doesn't work that way. Ask any CEO, including the President of the United States. You need to work on your peers and subordinates as well. Waving a letter from the executive suite and demanding cooperation is *not* an effective ploy. Get your peers and senior management involved and identified with the program.

There are several schools of thought on how to solicit and solidify the support of your management peers.

The Task Force or Committee

The task force or committee usually comes to mind first. A lot depends on your organization's culture, but I believe that very little gets done by committees acting as committees. However, by creating one, you may be able to get, at least ostensibly, the level of inter- and intraorganizational support you need to make the program fly.

If the committee is a cultural necessity, then go with the flow. Be ready to propose but not impose. The trick is to get them to agree with what you want and to believe they came up with the idea. Accept any good suggestions (and you will get some) and be generous in giving credit. You are building alliances and trying to solicit "buy-in."

Consider whether you want to chair the committee. It usually gives you more control, but you may want (or be required) to cede the chair to a more senior member of management. The odds are very good that most senior managers won't see the chair as a major contributor to career advancement, or if they do, they're relying on you to make them look good. Either way, you can play the situation to your advantage.

Take the time to educate the group, especially the chairperson, and try your best to get common agreement on what constitutes the business of the committee and how you achieve closure. Keep the scope narrow and feasible. Concentrate on project plans, goals, and objectives. Keep how-to mechanics to a minimum.

It's a thankless job, but make sure you or someone on your staff keeps the minutes. Busy people's memories can be poor, and it's to your advantage that the common memory be preserved, especially when you have gotten commitment or made some progress.

The Passive Committee

Another technique that sometimes works is what I call the passive committee, or the "comment and consent" role. This group seldom, if ever, meets, but it does review and approve circulated documents, usually authored by you (or your staff, if you have one). The positive side is that you probably maintain more control than you would with an active committee or task force. The negative side is that the process can take forever, and some members will be bottomless pits—losing everything you send them and swearing they never got it.

Do not circulate documents sequentially; you'll seldom get them back. Even if you do, you won't be able to interpret everyone's comments. Sequential reviewers tend to comment on or be swayed by the comments of preceding reviewers, and you'll get less and less valid and objective input on the document itself. Finally, make it clear that you are not going to be able to achieve perfect democracy and accept every suggestion and comment. You will get comments that are polar opposites. Worse yet, you may actually want a third alternative. Try to handle these off-line and only with the individuals concerned.

Perfecting the resulting planning document is less important than the spirit of cooperation and support you are trying to nurture. You can always issue an amendment or update at a later date. The objective is to get everyone pulling for the program, and they'll do that only if they feel comfortable. Are some compromises required? You bet! Compromise on security? Of course! Unless you are engaged in highly secure defense-related activities or a program in which loss of life or extreme damage is possible, you're going to be operating on a sliding scale anyway.

Justifying an IP Program

Justifying an IP program is not always easy. In fact, it can be darned difficult. However, I don't mean that you should avoid justification. In fact, if you can sell an IP program without justifying it, there's something wrong with the enterprise you serve. But if you can at all avoid it, try not to get caught up in a "direct cost of program compared to value of information protected" justification process.

Am I saying that IP programs are not directly justifiable? No! What I am suggesting is that very few organizations have a sufficiently sophisticated business system to put reliable direct costs and valuations on the information *itself*. It can be a messy and conflict-ridden process, and it takes you away from the fundamental purpose of information protection: to support the enterprise. Concentrate instead on the costs and revenue impact from loss of processing or compromise. It sounds almost the same, but the difference is critical. You may not know what the direct value of an accounts receivable record is, but you sure can measure the cash-flow impact if your receivables aren't processed for a week or become untrustworthy.

Try not to justify on the basis of avoiding a specific threat. If your customer service function is out of action, it doesn't matter whether it was caused by corrupted data, software failure, hardware failure, a hacker, a virus, or any combination. You have unhappy and possibly lost customers and revenue. Justify on the basis of business impact. You'll get less academic arguments and you'll arrive at agreement on priorities faster. Business impact justification is especially important in those areas in which return on investment (ROI) techniques are popular. Try to incorporate in your justification the intangible but real value of added **control** and discipline.

For example, if you decide that quality control of software development needs tightening up for security reasons—making sure programmers don't put processes and privileges into programs that don't belong there—remember that the added controls and tests required to carry that off could also result in a more stable, better-documented, easier to update, and easier to understand piece of software. That contributes directly toward processing productivity. Designing, developing, and deploying code rapidly is not a sign of programming success; designing, developing, and deploying efficient, cost-effective, and well-controlled code is. There's a big difference, and your security measures can make a contribution. There is a very strong affinity among quality, control, and security. Use it.

Some Final Advice

The most fundamental principle is: Know what you can reasonably do, and don't allow yourself to become overcommitted (or underresourced). Pressure to perform miracles within severe time and cost constraints can be very difficult to resist. But remember, the only thing worse than no IP program is a failed IP program. More programs fail from overly ambitious objectives and expectations than from poor execution. Here are a few caveats:

• Never bill an IP program as a one-shot deal. Never say, "Give me this and you'll never hear from me again." If you do, you'll be lying.

• Never bill a protection program as a total program. It won't be, and you wouldn't want it to be anyway.

• Don't tie the program to artificial deadlines. Management may give you the go-ahead provided the project is completed and the funds expended in this fiscal year. (The fiscal year usually has about sixty days left when these offers are made.) The temptation can be overwhelming, and it can be a great opportunity, if you can rescale the project to what you can reasonably do in the time allocated. Otherwise, you may be walking into a trap.

• Make sure the resources are available to do what you want. You need skills as well as funding, and they may not be immediately (or ever) available. I realize that you can get into a major double bind here: Many companies operate on a "no resource commitment without funds" basis, but funds are useless to you without resources to execute.

• This may sound insultingly fundamental, but make sure management really understands what you're doing. If management thinks bringing up an access control facility simply means purchasing and installing a piece of software, and you know it means a major administrative and technical initiative with ongoing costs and user impact, you have a bad case of false management expectations. Unless you fix it, you will regret it.

• Once you've been given the go-ahead, provide status reports with meaningful content. Telling management that 50 percent of the tasks are completed and 40 percent of the funds are expended doesn't tell it a thing. Use your status reports to renew and reinforce management's understanding of what you are doing, the purpose of the program, your current level of success, and any critical factors that it needs to address in order to help you succeed.

• Regarding project budgets and resources, remember that "management giveth and management taketh away." Let's face it. Unless your management is indeed exceptional or the auditors or regulators have been crawling all over your enterprise, your security project will seldom be classified as mandatory with inviolate funding. If your funds are provided on a discretionary basis, then be prepared for discretionary downsizing. Plan for what you can do at, say, 10 and 20 percent reduction levels. Don't advertise your reduced contingency plan, but if you adequately anticipate a reduction, you can usually survive it.

Make sure management understands that it will not be getting the same results and that some important functions are being delayed or abandoned. Otherwise, what did you need the full amount for in the first place? Stiff-upper-lip budget heroics can backfire badly. They can make it seem as though you overestimated your initial requirements and can severely damage your credibility. But I've also discovered that having a backup plan for budget reductions can help avoid deeper cuts. You can come across as a trustworthy steward of the enterprise's funds who is deserving of consideration the next time things loosen up. Obviously there is a point of no return. If you don't have enough funding to do anything meaningful, say so.

• Finally, remember that few members of your organization will be sharing the same level of enthusiasm you have for the program. A little occasional boosterism among your peers and subordinates can go a long way toward ensuring continued cooperation. Enthusiasm is ephemeral; it can disappear rapidly. Work toward maintaining it, especially among your allies. Don't get so caught up in knocking off the opposition that you forget to consolidate and ensure continued support from your friends.

7

Pre-Program Development Considerations

What's in this chapter?

- Ensuring a Business Orientation
- Fitting the Program to the Organization
- Getting Internal and External Help
- Knowing When to Stop
- Getting Staff Assistance

Getting management approval and peer support for an **information protection** (IP) program is an important step, and you will, no doubt, have to resolicit that support. The time has now come for turning proposals and concepts into fact.

Ensuring a Business Orientation

Throughout our discussions, I've been stressing that an IP program must be based on business objectives and business requirements because **information** is a business resource. (*Business* includes institutional and governmental functions.) Your plan should concentrate on the critical business functions that use information processing. It should be structured in terms of the effects that the loss of integrity, confidentiality, or availability of **information resources** will produce on those functions. It should offer preventive and reactive measures that have a business rationale. It should be business justified.

Unfortunately, many **security** and **continuity** programs start (and sometimes end) with the technology. It's easy to fall into that mode. After all, isn't it the technology that has really created the need for a protection program? If it weren't for computers and telecommunications, would we even be talking about the subject? Probably not. There is no doubt you should pay significant attention to technology, but your attention should be directed toward its impact on your enterprise.

In Chapter 6, I raised the prospect of an awareness program as an important opening step in putting your protection program together. One key side effect of this approach is to put early emphasis on the people and business aspects of your protection plan. It helps keep the priorities in their proper order.

The reason I'm stressing this point is to counter the common belief held by many business managers that information protection can be accomplished simply by waving money and technology at the issues. Many expensive protection programs founder because the management and user commitment never develops along with the technology, although there are exceptions. In an environment dominated by mainframe computers, it is possible to go a long way using very little but the technology and technologists. The users end up being controlled by management information systems (MIS) or data security department fiat. If the MIS department has a reasonably good sense of what's important and who should be using what, an enterprise could go on for years under that form of control.

There's nothing wrong with that, but times are changing. You, as a nontechnical manager, are getting involved in this process, probably because you have been put in charge (or have put yourself in charge) of some form of information processing technology. The odds are that the MIS department is only tangentially involved in what you're doing. Maybe it helped you select equipment and software and opened up paths to the mainframes and the wide area network. Other than that, you will probably never hear from MIS. Or you may come from an organization that never had and probably never will have an MIS department. Either way, you're in charge, and your principal reason for getting all that technology was not to satisfy a lifelong passion for electric trains. You bought it to *improve your business.* Therefore, your protection program should have the same purpose.

The other important reasons for the emphasis on a business orientation for your IP program center around the issues of justification, management cooperation and participation, and ensuring appropriate executive expectations (see Chapter 6). They all come a lot more easily if the program is stated in business terms, minus the technical jargon and mumbo-jumbo. Probably most important, your own comfort level will be higher. You talk business more easily than computer technology. (Unless, of course, you're a closet "techie" who always wanted to swap tales of bits and bytes with the rest of the code slingers at the Last Download Saloon.)

Fitting the Program to the Organization

Make sure it's your plan and your requirements. Don't borrow from an existing program just because it's there. In fact, even if you're setting up a program for one department, resist the temptation to make a wholesale copy of the information programs that other departments have put into place. Enterprise-wide standardization may be a corporate objective, and each department creating its own program from scratch would be an abysmal waste of time, effort, and resources, but make sure that anything you copy or borrow is really right for you and your environment before you use it. Resist the Mt. Everest syndrome: "Why did you use that?" "Because it was there!" The temptation to believe that an existing program is just right for you is extremely strong, especially when the alternative is creating one yourself. Let me give you a short example to illustrate my point.

Several years ago, through sheer coincidence, I had the opportunity to visit with the CFOs of two ethical drug companies in the United States within a matter of two or three days. We were talking generally about the same information protection topics and, in both cases, I asked the question: "What do you consider to be the most important information resources your company has that it must protect?" From the same executive position in similar companies in the same industry, you'd expect the same or a similar answer, right? Wrong!

One CFO zeroed right in on the company's technology and the proprietary formulas for its new and developing products. That was the lifeblood of the organization, in his mind, and its loss or compromise could seriously (and perhaps irretrievably) damage the enterprise.

His counterpart in the other company had a different view. He was rather sanguine about protecting product technology. Most of it, he claimed, was written up in technical journals, was protected by the patent process, and was tied up in the federal and international review process, which in his mind was tantamount to publishing it in the *New York Times*. What he wanted to protect was the company's pricing strategies, its bids and contracts, and its proprietary marketing materials.

Who was right? Darned if I know! I suspect they both were, to a point. I was surprised at first at the disparity where I had expected agreement. In retrospect, though, every company has its own view of its environment, marketplace, competition, goals, objectives, and the ways to achieve them. Why should they be consistent about what information resources need to be protected most? The same may be true to a lesser extent within departments.

The point of this illustration is that you and your organization are different from other organizations. You may ultimately end up using the same technologies as others do for protection, but how you use them, on what, and the management infrastructure that surrounds that usage may be dramatically different. Even if it's not, you should assure yourself that you fit the mold before you use the program, not the other way around.

Clearly, in each of the drug companies I visited, the information targeted for special protection was different. However, when it came to threats, they both seemed more concerned about disclosure than disruption or modification (although these were not excluded from their total concerns).

The point is very simple, really, but like most simple points, often ignored. Clearly examine and catalog your own priorities and requirements. Then determine how much of the security and continuity material already available applies to you. If you're lucky, a lot will, but don't push yourself into an inappropriate program just for the sake of completing the job. Since, sad to say, you probably want to get it over with as soon as possible and you don't expect much direct job satisfaction or recognition for what you are doing, the temptation to lift another program and make it yours will be very strong. Resist temptation.

Getting Internal and External Help

You've been very conscientious. You've done an analysis of the information resources you want to protect and the threats you think are most likely to befall them. You have a good idea of the types of protection you want and the extremes you want to avoid. You also have a good idea of some of the other constraints you have to satisfy, such as ease of use, processing speed and throughput, cost, operating and training limits, the human resources available to administer a program, the enterprise's attitude toward standards and policies, and your own time and energy. You've gotten a general go-ahead to design and present a program. Now what?

To get this far, you may have already taken advantage of several resources, but the following catalog lists them all for the sake of completeness. They may not all exist in your enterprise, or they may be combined or shared.

Internal

- Data security administration
- Continuity or contingency planning administration
- Internal audit
- MIS, including operations
- Network administration
- Local area network (LAN) administration
- Data and database administration (the first deals with policy, strategy, standards, and procedures for data representation, storage, and usage, including general naming conventions and methods and mechanisms to be used; the second deals with the actual day-to-day administration of files, database management systems, user authorization, library, and dictionary techniques)
- Applications development and package selection
- System development
- Change management
- Decision support
- Legal
- Human resources
- Risk management or insurance administration
- Physical security
- Administrative and office services
- Real estate and building management
- Contract management (especially if your protection program involves vendors and contract personnel)
- Public relations (especially if some of your activities affect the public and public organizations, regulators, stockholders, or the media)

External (Public Agencies Listed Apply to the United States)

- Information protection consultants
- External auditors
- Law enforcement, including the Justice Department's National Institute of Justice
- Related societies and associations
- Hardware and software manufacturers, including those specializing in information protection
- Backup and recovery service vendors
- Telecommunications and network service vendors
- Insurance companies
- The National Institute of Standards and Technology
- The National Security Agency's National Computer Security Center
- Conference providers and educational services
- Publications (industry, technology, and protection specialists, including several subscription services)

To develop an effective program, do you have to contact and use them all? Of course not. If you did, you'd never get finished (or started). Some of the internal groups may not exist in your organization; you may not be on speaking terms with some of them or regard their opinions and assistance as worth having. But unless you are the sole provider of information services in your organization and none of these other functions exist, you should make some contacts and get their input. You also need the support and cooperation from the other staffs. They won't ensure your success, but they can assist you greatly under the proper conditions.

If you are going to use outside help, make sure that all parties are talking the same language and understand and agree on the scope of their participation, mode of operation, form and amount of compensation, and the nature of the deliverables you are to receive. For everyone's protection, get it in writing. This applies especially to those informal agreements you might be tempted to strike up with a friend or acquaintance who has some information protection expertise. In fact, I believe that the closer the relationship, the more you need a written agreement. Reread it every now and again to refresh your memory and to ensure you're getting what you bargained for. On the other hand, nothing ruins a client-consultant relationship faster than the client who tries to squeeze additional services into the engagement under the original contract price.

Knowing When to Stop

There is a point (rather early on, actually) at which the information you continue to accumulate provides less and less incremental value for the space, time, and expense it requires. A sure sign that you've accumulated enough information is when all your sources begin to sound like they're cross-referencing each other or a select few. At that stage, you know you've probably reached a point of diminishing return on data gathering. In any event, you certainly should have initiated your action program by then.

Don't take that statement as a recommendation to go off half-cocked and unprepared. But since any program you develop should be implemented in small, manageable phases with ample provision for adjusting course, you can afford to begin without becoming the world's greatest expert. Although you should have a relatively clear idea of where you intend to go, you don't need a step-by-step road map of the entire journey in order to begin. You'll make alterations to the itinerary, anyway.

Getting Staff Assistance

As far as structuring your assistance goes, a task force or committee is a great way to get a lot of the staff opinions you need, while providing a mechanism for keeping most of the horses running in the same direction. Don't lose control of the process, however. If your prior experience leads you to be wary of committees, then use a one-on-one approach or the passive committee (see Chapter 6).

There's a subtle but useful point to be observed here. Let's assume that you are now in a development and implementation mode; that you have approval to at least start a protection program. If you are still using the services of the same committee or task force you used to develop and get approval for the original proposal, make sure that every member of the team (including you) understands that you are no longer in the proposal stage. You are now an *action* committee; different rules and objectives apply. Be especially careful of reopening decisions already made in agonizing detail. By all means, be flexible and open to changes in plans, but also insist that decisions made are decisions to be enforced and implemented. Otherwise, you'll rotate around dead center forever.

In some cases, in order to help the process, you might wish to disband and then reestablish and rename the committee or task force, changing the makeup of the group just enough to make a difference. Otherwise, you may find yourself covering proposal ground over and over again. Regrouping may also give you a chance to get rid of some troublesome committee members and to add some significant strengths.

You may also find that if you are planning to use outside help, such as consultants, they can be helpful additions to the committee process. They can act as additional resources, facilitators, commentators, or rapporteurs. You probably should not let them chair the group; this is your program, and you should retain leadership. When the consultants leave, you still have the project to manage.

8

Planning, Developing, and Implementing a Protection Program

What's in this chapter?

- The Phased Approach
- The Basic Process
  —The Assessment Steps
  —The Implementation Steps

In developing an **information protection** (IP) program, take a phased approach and give yourself plenty of time. Most of us get into time binds as a result of making unfulfillable promises to management, succumbing to the pressure of "use it or lose it" budgets, or just plain underestimation of the time and effort that goes into making an effective program. Don't fall into those traps.

The Phased Approach

It may be that you have been temporarily assigned to this project and you want to get it off your back and get back to doing what you're getting paid for. If that's the case, your first job should be naming a *permanent* program manager. The manager responsible for *running* the program should help *develop* the program, if at all possible. This is not necessarily a *full-time* permanent program manager; full or part time is a call you can make as the program develops.

You are putting a process into place, not an event. There are no completion dates for an IP program—only start dates. Phases may end; the program doesn't. There are grades and stages of protection. Although only one grade may be ideal for your organization, a lesser grade can still be valuable. Aim for the ideal, but consider the intermediate stages as valuable and worth developing.

Total protection is not the ideal state. The minute the cost of protection exceeds the value of that which is being protected, you're into overkill, waste, and counterproductivity. The trick is figuring out the true value of what you're protecting in order to measure the ideal level of **security.** That step, asset valuation of **information resources** and processes, coupled with threat analysis, represent the most judgmental parts of a protection program. By comparison, developing and executing the mechanics are easy.

Another common error in developing and scheduling IP programs is to put the technological processes on the critical path and treat the management and administrative spadework and infrastructure as side issues. *The reverse is usually true.* This reversal of priorities is especially likely if a management information systems (MIS) technologist is in charge of the program. Getting a mainframe-based access control facility such as Computer Associates' ACF2 or Top Secret or IBM's RACF installed becomes the primary target and, in some cases, becomes the entire IP program.

When I ask clients to describe their information security programs, I often get the answer: "We have Product X installed."

"And?" I reply.

"And what? That's all we have installed!"

"That's not what I mean. Describe the rest of the program."

"What's to describe?"

Answer: Plenty.

There are three different types of phasing, and a lot depends on how information processing works in your organization. The variations are:

1. *Functional phasing.* Essentially, functional phasing involves a series of steps, each of which is carried out throughout the entire target organization before the next step is taken. For example, you complete enterprise-wide awareness programs and classification before embarking on further security and **continuity** steps.
2. *Organizational phasing.* With organizational phasing, you complete the whole process in one organizational unit before going on to the next.

3. *Hybrid phasing.* This is a combination of the first two and can appear in a myriad of variations.

There are other techniques, such as overlapping certain activities, that will probably make themselves apparent to you as you plan. If you have access to a project management software package, use it to lay out an information protection program. Don't get enslaved by it, but use it to define the steps, estimate time and resources, and identify critical points and dependencies.

Which approach you use is primarily a function of how autonomous or interdependent your organizational units are. If every department and division shares the same databases, then you'd better use functional phasing and get data administration and classification in place across that universe. If everyone's synchronized in information usage and sharing, then you have to bring security and continuity up in a synchronized fashion. Try to reduce the scope everywhere you can, however. Mass cutovers to a new system are never very pretty, no matter how well planned and developed they are. They can be done, and are done frequently, but they require lots of care, simulation, testing, and contingency plans to reverse the process if it's not working.

By comparison, piloting a small but typical organization from start to finish can have a number of advantages. You minimize disruption, you learn and improve the process, and you can formalize as you go. It could take longer, but not necessarily. If you have an option, examine this one—organizational phasing—first.

Even if you use organizational phasing, some level of functional phasing will take place within the target organization. For example, applying access control to a local area network (LAN) server affects all the LAN users simultaneously. But if only a handful of **applications, systems,** processors, users, and owners are involved, the process is still much easier to control.

The Basic Process

Before I begin, let me describe the ground rules I'm adopting:

- In order to provide a complete sequence of events, I am assuming you are starting from scratch.

- There is some flexibility in the order of events. I make note of those sequences that should be considered immutable.
- I treat security- and continuity-related steps together when it makes sense and separately when necessary.
- Certain of the steps require the services of technicians. When the technical parts come up, I describe what needs to be done and who is best able to do it for you.

The early steps of the program consist of fact gathering and assessment. The later steps are primarily implementation activities. You may wish to divide the program into these two categories and further subcategorize by types of common activities.

During the process, you may be tempted to treat certain steps as already performed or stipulated. For example, why perform Steps 1 and 2, identify the organizational scope and the information resources, when you have a top management edict to get purchasing squared away? Doesn't that pretty much spell it out? Not really! To pursue the example, purchasing is seldom a system entirely unto itself. Make sure the connections and dependencies are understood. To square away purchasing, you may have to deal with payables and perhaps the entire financial system. By all means, take advantage of legitimate shortcuts; just make sure they are legitimate.

You probably won't have total freedom of action, and certain steps may be accelerated or delayed because of management mandates, resource constraints, or external deadlines. Managers get paid for making the judgments that aren't in the book. You, of course, will decide whether you need every step I outline, but at least evaluate objectively why you are dropping certain steps. You may have to cycle back through some steps, changing the scope, ground rules, or results. That's normal. The process is not entirely linear. Nor will you get everything to your satisfaction first time out.

The Assessment Steps

Step 1. Identify the organizational scope to be addressed by the program. Will you deal with the entire enterprise, your division, department, related departments, or even multiple enterprises involved in common information usage? It sounds basic, but I've been engaged on several consulting assignments where this became a major bone of contention, especially over budget issues. Assuming you make exclusions, how will you eventually handle the excluded organizations?

Step 2. Identify, generically, within the organizational scope decided in Step 1, those information resources to be addressed by the program. Will you, for example, include manual handling of information, voice networks, fax networks, portable micros, micros in the home, external services? How will you eventually handle the exclusions?

Step 3. Determine whether there are incompatibilities between the outputs of Steps 1 and 2. For example, if you have identified your own department as the target but you depend on several other organizations for most of your computer and network support, or other departments own the databases you use, it's time to widen the scope and develop alliances.

Step 4. Identify, specifically, the resources to be considered in Steps 9 and 10—asset valuation and **risk assessment:** processing environments, systems (hardware and software), applications, files, shared views of data, communications.

Step 5. Identify the owners, users, and suppliers of services associated with the resources you have identified. Try to be as specific as possible about the functions each one performs. For example, if a database administrator exists and determines all the conventions for naming data and other resources, including supplying the names themselves, that is important to note and to use.

Step 6. Under this step, identify other organizations that may be involved and the nature of their involvement. If, for example, you need to develop a unique user identification code (not a password), do the human resources and accounting departments have to agree? What are your options?

Step 7. Determine who has to approve your program in both its preliminary and finished form. They may not be the same players. Include both line management and relevant staffs. This is always a problem. You may be opening Pandora's box by soliciting "approvers," especially if they have reputations for being "disapprovers." On the other hand, you may be inviting a major shoot-out if the program comes as a surprise to operating groups and management that have legitimate claims on sign-off. You know your organization's politics better than I do.

Step 8. Solicit approval for initial stages. If you didn't do this before the program began, don't go any further without generally outlining your *initial* program and seeking management approval.

Until now, you've been scoping what you want to do and building the contents of a plan. You are about to get into the steps that require more significant time and effort.

Now that you've defined the organizational and functional scope of the program, go through the rest of this outline, selecting the initial steps you will perform, roughly estimating the time involved and the cost ranges. Unless you have to do otherwise, limit yourself to the early stages of the program—fact finding and design. Obviously, at this stage, judging time and cost for the detailed implementation will be a rather broad estimate (wild guess). Consultants and others with experience can assist you in making estimates, if necessary.

Since you have not yet conducted any type of risk assessment or asset valuation (that's next), you will have to use your intuitive judgment coupled with your experience to come up with a general description of what you're seeking to protect and what threats you're trying to prevent.

Don't be embarrassed by the fact that you have little hard data at this stage. What you are saying essentially is: "Based on my observations and experience as a manager, I have reason to believe that certain of the information resources could be in jeopardy. These, in turn, could put our enterprise in jeopardy. I want the authorization to pursue that belief further and to develop a set of appropriate information protection recommendations. If further action is not justified, we have the benefits of an assessment to support that decision. If action is justified, this will help us make the right decisions."

The variables that will most greatly affect your costs are:

- Number of organizations to be covered.
- Number and type of information resources.
- Number of processing environments and locations. (One data center may be easier to evaluate than twelve local area networks (LANs) unless they are absolute clones, and distance will, of course, have a bearing.)
- Number and variety of system **platforms.** (IBM does it differently from DEC from HP from Unisys; even within IBM's product line, there are significant differences in platform design and security function.)
- Number of applications and files. If most applications share the same generalized database or each application has its own captive

files, the process isn't that difficult. If, as is the usual case, the truth lies somewhere in between, more analysis is necessary. For certain complex applications, you may want to go down to the transaction and data view level. This will be the case during implementation, because each transaction *may* have a different protection pattern. It may not be necessary for assessment purposes, however.

- Number of users, owners, and service suppliers.

- Complexity and scope of any networks involved.

- The support structure available to you, ranging from word-processing and secretarial support to readily available descriptions of the items mentioned above. Updated, accurate documentation is worth its weight in titanium. Unfortunately, even in the most sophisticated of enterprises, it is in woefully short supply. Therefore, plan on documenting everything you do; you will not regret it.

Step 9. Select an asset (resource) valuation mode. Don't let the formality of that statement put you off. I'm simply talking about reaching a level of agreement on how to prioritize the family jewels. The approach that is most effective is a business impact analysis. Which resources do you regard as most critical to run your enterprise? Which ones must you have available to carry out your mission? Which ones must you preserve from fraud and unauthorized change? Which ones could be harmful if disclosed?

I have a strong aversion to using tangible asset valuation techniques to answer these questions. Have you ever tried to depreciate a database? It can be done, but it's not my idea of a fun time. In fact, if the term *asset* starts moving you in that direction, switch to *resource.*

Step 10. Select your risk assessment mode (you may also hear this called threat analysis). Here's one of the first areas in which you have to choose whether you're going to cover security, continuity, or both. I hope you opt for both. Having defined and prioritized the resources or assets we consider to be of value, we now try to ascertain some level of risk associated with those resources.

This is actually a two-stage activity: You are trying to ascertain *what* will happen and the *likelihood* of it happening. The *impact* of the event is developed in Step 11, but it is a fairly natural fallout of Steps 9 and 10. The types of threats you deal with and their probability will be affected by your choice to deal with security or continuity.

Generally speaking, there is more hard data on physical threats such as fire, water, storm, and infrastructural failure. There has been a lot written but little scientifically proven on the frequency of logical threats such as hacker attacks, computer fraud, viruses, and the like. The reason is simple. Physical threats are more visible and easier to count and describe. When Wall Street had its blackout or San Francisco its earthquake, you didn't have to go far to get the details of the impact.

On the other hand, logical attacks are often more subtle. They are not usually published by the victim for many reasons, not the least of which is self-defense. If you have a vulnerability, you usually don't advertise it. The attacks that get into the courts are a relatively small proportion of the total, but I openly admit that I don't know what the total is.

The saving grace in this situation is that for many types of information resources, one hit is too many. Even if you don't live in a high crime area, having a sable coat in the front closet may be enough reason for a burglar alarm. The message is: Keep the risk assessment process in perspective.

Step 11. Do a vulnerability assessment. This sounds like a risk assessment, and sometimes they're combined, but there is a difference. Here what you're doing is assessing the value of the protective measures you already have in place against the risks you've defined. Let's follow it through with an example:

USGUYS has a critical system that must stay on the air to serve its clients (asset or resource valuation). The building is in an active earthquake zone (risk assessment), but it meets earthquake resistance specifications. USGUYS has backup power and communications, but they're all at this site and could go with the quake (vulnerability assessment). Therefore, USGUYS has some exposure.

Some organizations roll Steps 9, 10, and 11 into one package. The level of formality is a matter of management style and available time and resources. How you package it is your concern. Just make sure you go through the process.

Step 12. This is the final step for data gathering and assessment, and it's related to Step 11. I call it a data security and continuity function assessment. What have you got in the way of overall protective measures, organization, infrastructure? This step is included to catch all the generic measures you have in place that may not necessarily surface in the assessment of any individual threat or vulnerability. Include activities such as internal audit, general security, and any specific initiatives originated in individual departments. Take note of any policies, guidelines, and standards that could have a bearing on what you're doing. In short, it's a quick inventory of whatever else may be in the arsenal that you can use in the implementation steps that follow.

Step 13. Now it's decision time. Organize the output of your assessments and determine whether there is sufficient reason to develop additional protective measures. If the value, risk, and vulnerability are sufficient, it's time to present your findings to management for its approval and the resources to go on.

The Implementation Steps

Overwhelming as the assessment stage might seem on first reading, if you sit down and apply it to your own situation, you will probably find that it is well within the range of feasibility, especially if you keep the size of the universe you're dealing with reasonable. Can an information protection start-up run into hundreds of thousands or millions of dollars? Yes, but it seldom does. Viewed from a different perspective, most organizations spend less than 3 or 4 percent of their total information processing budget on information protection. In many companies, that's in the spillage range.

You're going to find less straight-line progression in the implementation steps than you did in assessment. In assessment, you were trying to develop a set of conclusions and recommendations. With implementation, there is a general sequence to the process, but there is more flexibility in how it is carried out.

You are also going to find a certain amount of data gathering and assessment in the implementation steps. That doesn't mean you did a poor job during assessment. It means that, having established a need, you now require more detailed information in order to bring the program to fruition. Getting some of this information prior to beginning the program probably wouldn't have been worth the effort.

Step 1. First comes policy, standards, and guidelines (procedures) development. An IP policy is the bedrock on which the program should be built. However, it is highly dependent on the culture of the organization. Some enterprises are awash in policy statements; others have none. I continue to be surprised by the number of organizations that do not believe in policies, but I confess to being biased, having come from a policy-dominant company like IBM.

Policies look different to different companies. They should be a set of high-level statements of direction and guidance, not detailed how-to efforts. The how-to belongs in standards, guidelines, or procedures. I have seen IP policies as short as half a page and as long as twenty or thirty pages. Somewhere in between is probably right.

Finally, standards and guidelines should develop as the rest of the program develops. Don't sit down to write all of the guidance up front; let it evolve with the program. Write and circulate drafts. You'll need them.

Step 2. Develop an awareness program (see Chapters 6 and 15). You can develop and present an awareness program at various stages and for various purposes: to gain management and employee support for future initiatives, to kick off parts of the program, to raise levels of general sensitivity for its own sake. Think in terms of several levels and types of awareness programs.

Don't take the placement of this step literally. It should follow the development of your policies and basic guidance so you have something to communicate to the organization, but it can take place later in the process, several times during the process, and on a recurring basis for different audiences.

Step 3. Develop a strategy and architecture. Strategies and architectures sound like high-class "techie-talk." Perhaps, but there is a great deal of management and administrative content in every one of them. Business strategies shouldn't bother you. You probably cut your teeth on them.

An architecture is simply a means of ensuring that things work together consistently, effectively, and seamlessly. A security strategy might be stated as follows:

- Balancing preventive versus reactive measures
- Centralized or decentralized control
- Balancing administrative versus technological controls
- Bottom-up or top-down design

The outcome of a security or continuity strategy is a set of requirements that is, in turn, fulfilled by detailed implementation. There is a hidden catch here, however. Information protection strategies and architectures *cannot be developed in isolation*. They must support the information processing strategies and architectures, which must, in turn, support the business goals and objectives. This means that in order to develop an IP strategy and architecture, you must have access to, knowledge of, and understanding of the wider range of strategies and architectures. If your company is going to a centralized shared data architecture for all end users, your security and continuity concerns will be vastly different than if each database were directly owned by an application. This is one of those cases requiring more data gathering.

Step 4. Develop requirements. These come in several dimensions:

- Security and continuity
- Administrative and technical
- Generic and specific

Step 5. Consider the detailed implementation of the program. On the technical side, this may involve developing or acquiring software. On both the technical and administrative sides, it involves standards, procedures, guidelines, budgeting, staffing, and establishment of functions.

Step 6. Determine how to handle ongoing program management; how to handle the steady state. (See Chapter 11 for more details.)

Step 7. Consider the measurement, audit, and quality control of the security and continuity process. Don't leave this one out. It includes such things as testing your contingency plans, auditing violations, checking on security privileges being granted, periodically checking the software development process, and other important pressure points. Don't leave this step to the end. As you develop a program, determine how you are going to measure it and make sure that it's measurable.

There are further refinements to each of these steps. Setting up liaisons with other departments such as legal, human relations, public relations, and crisis management is part of the process. If you are in a regulated industry, dealing with the regulators may be a separate effort all its own.

I hope I haven't overwhelmed you. Clearly, this is a program that evolves. You will reap benefits at the intermediate stages, and the expenditures need not be out of line. However, if your organization has spent little or nothing up to this point, moving from zero is always the greatest issue. Inertia can be difficult to deal with.

I have laid the whole program before you so you can observe its totality. Plan and implement incrementally. It has been done and is being done by a large number of organizations and executives who, like you, have come to the realization that information has become too important to leave uncontrolled and unprotected.

9

Elements of an Information Security Program

This chapter and Chapter 10 cover the two components of **information protection** separately: security and continuity. The primary purpose of an information **security** program is to allow authorized persons and processes to do what they are supposed to do and to prevent everything else. The shorthand term that is often used is *access control.* But there's a bit more to information security than access control.

The term *authorized processes* is included in the statement above because it's common in today's information **systems** for one transaction to trigger another and to continue in a daisy chain. Order entry can automatically trigger credit, salesperson commission, invoice, accounts receivable, production, and possibly even shipping transactions in a highly integrated system.

Authorized *persons* may not always be aware of the complete transaction chain they have set off. Access control must be designed to cover such cause-and-effect relationships, or it will be in danger of being bypassed or compromised by hidden transactions.

Access Control Mechanisms

Access control is fundamental to the security process. If you are protecting against disruption, modification, disclosure, or use of **information resources,** then you must be able to control, *to the extent necessary,* access to those resources. For those of you who have ever taken a journalism or writing course, this is a good time to review the basic elements of any good story: Who? What? When? Where? How? Why? They apply here.

An access mechanism may be a guard at a door. It could be a key card or similar tool for entry into an area or device such as an automatic teller machine. Computer access control facilities are usually a combination of software and administrative procedures. Lately, specific hardware devices have become available to assist in the process.

All access control mechanisms must do the same basic things. They must determine:

1. Who is authorized to access the system, **information,** or resources in question.
2. What they are authorized to do.
3. How they are authorized to do it.
4. What specific parts or aspects of the resource they can access.
5. Under what circumstances they can access them.

Then the access control mechanism must control the person's or processes' activities accordingly.

You may have noticed that the list doesn't include why the person or process is there. That's because the access control mechanism can't ask the individual or transaction and assume that it will get a straight answer. What would a hacker say? So it makes an assumption based on rules supplied by management. If the mechanism can't identify an individual, should it assume that a "hostile" is trying to break in and raise the alarm? Or should it assume that an authorized user is having trouble and, therefore, refuse to admit the person or process and simply log the event and pass on? You supply the operating assumptions.

In the least stringent case, you can set the mechanism to note the discrepancy and still let the caller in. This option is supplied to give managers some latitude on how rapidly they go to full, active control during the early days of installation. After all, you installed your computer to do useful work, and you don't want to shut down completely while you determine whether your electronic watchdog is nearsighted or not. These systems typically need some time to get all the authorizations, identifications, and rules straight. This option helps, but make sure it gets upgraded at the appropriate time, or you're wasting your time and money on a completely passive system.

Consider the following access control statement: *You* are authorized to *make queries* into the *payroll files.* This one's not specific enough; it doesn't take care of all the elements. In order to satisfy the five requirements I listed previously, you need a more detailed statement, such as:

1. You, after providing the appropriate unique identification code and password,
2. Are authorized to make queries,
3. Only through the payroll inquiry application facility,
4. Of the nonsalary fields of the payroll records,
5. From an authorized workstation only during the prime shift.

There are a lot of conditions and implied restrictions in that statement. Let's examine them:

1. *You, after providing the appropriate unique identification code and password.* . . . You need both a unique identifier (ID) and a password. The ID is usually assigned to you, usually doesn't change, and may be commonly known throughout the system, since it's often used for other purposes such as accounting for the computer time you use. The password is also unique to you, but normally is created by you, can and should be periodically changed, and should be known only to you and the facility that's challenging you. It's possible to have common group IDs and passwords if operational needs require them, but your security will be weaker as a result.

2. . . . *are authorized to make queries.* . . . You can't modify a record, add new records, delete, or do anything else.

3. . . . *only through the payroll inquiry application facility* . . . and no other means. Writing your own little query program is out; copying the contents of the database is off limits; using a backup facility to get a copy is unauthorized.

4. . . . *of the nonsalary fields of the payroll records.* . . . You can gather indicative information, hours worked, statistics, and other such information. Approaches to detailed or summary salary fields will be blocked.

5. . . . *from an authorized workstation only during the prime shift.* Forget about dialing up from a hotel or your home unless it's authorized. Working Sundays or off-shift on the payroll file is regarded as inappropriate.

This example in English can be translated into codes or rules understood by a software access control facility such as IBM's Resource Access Control Facility (RACF) or Computer Associates' two offerings, Top Secret and ACF2 for IBM systems using the MVS or VM operating systems. Other access control systems have similar structures. They perform the same essential functions, but like all hardware and software, they have functional, capacity, price, and performance differences. Some vendors such as Digital Equipment and Tandem package access control right into their operating systems. Some packaged **applications** and database management programs contain their own access control.

Obviously, this was only an example. Rules differ with each circumstance, but they should all address the five elements presented above, even if only to say that there are no restrictions. One individual may have dozens of rules governing what he or she is allowed to do. Similarly, a single resource—for example, a payroll file—may have an accumulation of rules governing all the persons and transactions that can access it, under what circumstances, through what facilities, to what extent, and to do what. From one perspective, you look at all the authorizations held by an individual or a process. From another, you look at all the individuals and processes with authorized access to a given resource. Both perspectives are important for security.

If all of these rules and descriptions have you wondering whether it's worth it, you should know that a lot of this process can be minimized. For example, the odds are good that every order entry or payroll administrator will have the same rules. Second, you usually phase in one application after another. Third, there are software assists to help in rule writing. Fourth, there are folks like me who assist in this process for a living. You cannot and should not try to bring an access control process up overnight. It's a learning and development process as well as a protective process.

How Does Access Control Work?

The access control process is made up of the following elements: authorization, identification and verification, controlled access, accountability, and auditability.

Authorization

The authorization process is the companion to classification (see Chapter 3). Under classification, you determine how you want to control access to the data. Here, you determine who will be granted that access and under what conditions. Two principles apply:

1. *Need to know,* which addresses confidentiality.
2. *Level of least privilege,* which addresses integrity.

In both instances, the selection process is business driven. What do you need to access for purposes of reading (need to know) or creating, modifying, or destroying (level of least privilege)? In each case, the object is to authorize your access to only those data you require to do your job and allow you to perform only those functions and processes on those data that are required to do your job.

This is largely an administrative process. Regardless of how you classify or don't classify your information and information resources, you are going to have some criteria for making authorization decisions. It may be management intuition, or it may be the result of a formal and rigorous **risk assessment.** It may say that *any* person with a certain job description can see and do certain things. It may be far more specific to *each* person based on a carefully negotiated need to know. The process differs.

Somebody has to administer the authorization process. It consists of getting specific or blanket written authorization from the information owner and developing software rules from that authorization. A typical blanket statement would automatically authorize all members of a department by virtue of their jobs to perform certain functions on certain resources.

Identification and Verification

Identification is next. Who are you? Your unique user ID usually provides preliminary information. You may have some supplemental identifier—*not the password*—to assist. The system searches its files to determine whether your ID is authorized for the resources you are signing on to. The system doesn't know who you are yet; all it knows is that the ID you're using is OK. Now it has to make sure you're using your own ID. (A similar process applies to automatically generated transactions.)

Verification is the next step. Who are you really? Are you some person off the street who guessed or stole an authorized user's identifier? Are you someone else in the department who knows it? Here's where a password or an equivalent device provides verification.

Passwords

Let's say you have a personal computer (PC) connected to a local area network (LAN). Let's assume that you have identified yourself to the system through your user ID. This process is often automatic on terminals and PCs. When you first boot up your computer, workstation, or terminal, very frequently a menu program appears on your screen. That menu program offers you the choice of logging on as yourself or allows guests using your machine to log on as themselves. By pressing the appropriate key, your ID is forwarded to the LAN management software, which in turn responds with a request for verification. Today, ninety-nine chances out of one hundred, it asks for your password.

Unlike the ID, passwords should be kept strictly between the user and the access control facility and should be changed often. You usually get your first password assigned to you when you are first authorized, in order to start the process. The first thing you should do is change it to something else that fits the ground rules established by management.

If you've had any experience with access control systems, you've probably used a password. If you're typical of the computer-using population, you've also probably misused a password. I don't mean you've deliberately compromised security; I simply mean that passwords can be a pain in the neck to both the user and the information security administrator and, as a result, we often shortcut good password practice. There are new techniques on the market that, I hope, will eventually make the *reusable* password (the one you and I normally encounter) obsolete.

However, even reusable passwords can be improved in a number of ways. Generally, you are trying to create a verification object that is strong enough to resist guessing or breaking by a reasonably adept individual with less than fanatic determination. You are not trying to make your system KGB proof. You want to make the effort to break in greater than most people are willing to expend. Once you pass that point, you're into overkill and endangering your own ability to use the password.

The first way to improve passwords is by making them inherently stronger:

• Start by using alphabetic as well as numeric characters. By using alphanumerics, you substantially increase the number of combinations available. Don't use alphabetics alone.

• Choose an effective password length. A computer program for guessing passwords can come up with every combination of three alphanumeric characters in a matter of minutes. A password of five to seven characters, which is the length usually recommended, takes a great deal longer (and then, of course, you have to try each one).

• Choose passwords that are not inherently weak such as all one number or letter or alternate letters. Don't use current dates. The number combination 199X gives away over half your password.

• Don't get personal, at least with information other people would know, such as your spouse's or pet's name, your license plate number, phone number, office room number, hobbies, interests, and so on. Remember, the odds are quite good that people who try to get into your system have easy physical access to it. These are usually people who know you. Not all attacks come from hackers in some remote location.

• Choose a password that doesn't make any sense, to you or anyone else. However, you have to be able to remember the password yourself, or else you may resort to that violation of violations, writing your password down and keeping it where you (and someone else) can find it. If you can develop easily remembered gibberish, go to it. Just don't lock yourself out along with everyone else. There are several programs on the market that generate random passwords of desired strengths. You may want to investigate one or two of them.

The second way to improve passwords is to improve password discipline:

• Don't write them down and don't put them in obvious places. It sounds silly, but I have seen passwords stuck to the sides and front of display screens. It's the equivalent of leaving your house key under the welcome mat.

• Change passwords often. Some organizations require changes every thirty or forty-five days. The system automatically informs you that your password has expired and insists that you supply a new one before it will let you go any further.

• Don't reuse old passwords. Some access control facilities keep a record of previously used passwords and won't let you reuse one for a year or so. If you're concerned, the access control facility usually encrypts all of its stored passwords so that someone with access to it can't uncover everyone else's passwords.

• Limit the number of attempts the access control system will accept and then lock the individual (the user ID) out. Depending on the circumstances, you may require some management intervention before that ID is reactivated. If the attacker can just wait a few minutes and renew the process, the lockout function is ineffective.

Can a security administrator see your password? In most systems, no. If you forget your password, you can be assigned a temporary one to get you back on the system. You must then change that password to a new one that only you and the access control software will know. To get a temporary password, you normally must identify yourself to the security administrator's satisfaction. If your access privileges include high-risk resources, you may need your management's approval. These kinds of optional procedures are part of the security decisions each enterprise has to make for itself, balancing administrative overhead and cost against level of security desired.

A third way to improve passwords is to use a relatively new technique: the one-time password. A major part of the conventional password's vulnerability (but also its usefulness) is the fact that it's reusable. If someone gets your password, he or she can use it as long as it's valid. There is a way around this problem.

One of the most difficult forms of cipher to break is the one-time code. The most basic form of one-time code is the code book—page after page of different substitutions for letters and numbers. When you send a message, you indicate (usually separately and clandestinely) the page number in the code book you're going to use. The recipient uses the same page to decode the message. Then you both destroy that page from the code book.

There is an equivalent type of one-time password that requires the use of a device and special software. It combines what you know with what you have. The individual products on the market differ a little from one another in detail, but fundamentally you carry a "token"—a little device that can look like a credit card, a calculator, or a key-chain attachment. Each one is unique. This token is part of the access verification process. It may also double as a badge for physical entry.

You identify yourself to the system you are trying to access and you also identify the token you carry. The system transmits a challenge number, phrase, or, in one case, a stream of blips on the screen that are read directly by the token. You enter the challenge into your token or device and it gives you a number or phrase with which to respond to the access control system. When you enter the correct response number or phrase, the system grants you access.

The system and the token are synchronized with each other (usually through a method known only to the manufacturer). The one-time password eliminates much of the need for password memorization. It is nontransferrable in the sense that if you lose the token, you know it's gone. If someone finds out your conventional password, you may never know it. Even if someone finds or steals your token, it still requires an ID and PIN (personal identification number), just like an automatic teller machine, to activate the process. To break into the system using your token, the individual must know your user ID and your special PIN, have the token, and, of course, attempt to access the appropriate system on the other end. Foolproof? No! Effective? Yes! Stronger than a conventional password? Much! More complex and expensive? Yes! But not that much, if the information resources are worth it. Consider using one-time passwords for special systems and applications where extra strength is needed.

Other Verification Devices

The general means of verifying your identity to someone (or a process) is by demonstrating a unique characteristic that you've agreed upon earlier. The degree of uniqueness and strength varies with the types of identifying objects or techniques used. These usually are:

• *Something you know.* This can be a password, your mother's maiden name, your last credit card balance, or the secret handshake of the Order of the Prairie Dog. Clearly, these can all be compromised or may not be uniquely yours in the first place. Your family and friends probably know your mother's maiden name. But for certain limited-risk activities, they suffice.

• *Something you have.* This might be a key, badge, or token. These may start out life as unique, but if lost or copied, they may be compromised. Some tokens are difficult, if not impossible, to copy.

• *Something you are.* This can be your voice, retina configuration, finger or palm print, or signature ballistics. We sign our names automatically, repeating the same general pressure, changes of directions, and pauses. Although an expert forger can reproduce the configuration of your signature, the forger usually cannot reproduce the dynamics. There are devices that can measure and check the ballistics (dynamics) of your signature with high reliability. They require that you sign your name some twenty or thirty times to establish a statistical picture of the signature dynamics. After that you must sign on with a special pen that measures pressure and other ballistic characteristics.

All of these techniques that verify on the basis of personal characteristics are usually categorized as *biometric*. Biometric systems can, in most cases, provide much better than average verification. However, they are often bulky and expensive, and probably will never reach the same low cost per workstation that a password provides. They are not all that socially acceptable either. Many people resist being fingerprinted. They object to anything having to do with the eye and resent personal registration processes such as that required for signature dynamics verification.

However, a useful security strategy can be developed by using combinations of the above verification techniques based on the individual security requirements of the information resources being accessed. Passwords may suffice for baseline protection, but for transactions above a certain amount, or access to restricted data, a second or third technique may be added.

Controlled Access

After identification and verification comes the actual controlled access process. You are now being let in. To where? This is the other major element of design and management decision besides authorization. Access control works only if the transactions to be controlled are placed under the access control facility's supervision. Technically, this is not a big deal, but it does require some understanding of how the specific application is designed and accepts incoming traffic, which is usually pretty straightforward.

What can be a little trickier is ensuring that there are no other paths into the application, system, or resource you are protecting. This is referred to as system or application integrity. If there's an open back door or no walls, you could be wasting a lot of time and resources protecting the front door.

Unless you are technically astute and experienced, you are going to have to rely to a large extent on the designers and programmers of your applications to ensure that back doors don't exist or, if they do, that they are kept closed and locked. You may want to get that assurance in writing and make them explain how the system or application attains integrity in words you understand. Technical jargon, as you well know, can often be a smoke screen to hide the speaker's lack of knowledge.

Integrity is important. Lack of integrity amounts to an open door for hackers and viruses to get into systems and applications. If the resources you're protecting are important enough, you may want to get some outside help from professionals who break into systems (legally) to ensure that your system and applications have integrity.

Administering controlled access is another consideration. What do you do with a violation? Record it by all means. But what happens after you record it? Do you block the transaction? Do you let it through? If someone fails to sign on correctly, how many tries does he or she get? What happens then? Some companies establish procedures that block access until a senior manager reinstates the individual in writing. That may be appropriate, but how much productive time has gone down the drain in the process? If the "offender" is a major customer, are you going to make that individual wait twenty-four hours for written authorization? I doubt it. You may need a hot-line number.

The reason I'm asking the questions and not answering them is that they are business decisions that you must make to fit your situation. Access control facilities are designed with a wide range of administrative options. The ones you choose must be the best balance between caution and the realities of your business or institution. Don't roll over and play dead, but don't go into overkill either.

Accountability

Accountability means that a process exists to connect an individual with an action. The passwords, IDs, and rules are the connecting links. Most access control systems have a logging and reporting function. Where those reports go (if they are ever generated), what actions are taken, and by whom are important administrative processes and are part of access control.

All violations should be reported back to the information resource owner for final disposition. Statistics maintained by the access control facility should be reviewed, understood, and acted upon. If a large number of violations are coming from a specific department, there may be a management problem, a lack of understanding of the system, a problem with the rules, or a technical problem with the system. Don't jump to conclusions until you've investigated.

If no violations are being reported, especially early in the process, you may also have a problem. No system is perfect. Yours may have been improperly set up. Unfortunately, that's more difficult to find.

Over the long haul, if your system is continually reporting a significant number of violations, your overall security program (not just access control) isn't working. Either your people are improperly trained or improperly motivated, or there is a mismatch between the security rules and the activities going on in your system. A high body count is not the sign of a good security program.

One other point to consider: In this age of the microprocessor, workstation, and intelligent terminal, it's easy to assume that most information processing is interactive, that is, direct processing between an individual user and the system. That's not necessarily true! There's still plenty of batch processing around—that is, the old mode of submitting a program (and data) to be run as part of a job stream and getting the results back from the data center. Oddly enough, in many organizations, even though it is still the primary way of running information processing applications, batch processing does not receive the security attention it deserves. It's often easy to enter programs and data into a batch job stream even though interactive access from a terminal is being carefully controlled. That's something to check!

Auditability

This is a distinct characteristic related both to security and accounting controls. It means having the ability to reconstruct an event or process. Accountability deals with who is responsible. Auditability seeks to determine what actually happened. The major tools are process documentation, logs and journals, and the use of unambiguous identification and verification techniques.

Other Information Security Techniques

There are other techniques related to access control, and they fall under the general category of resource integrity. As I mentioned before, back doors can exist in systems and applications. How do they get there? They are either designed in deliberately or result from less-than-optimum design and implementation.

Deliberate back doors are not always signs of unethical behavior. Some designers put them there for legitimate test and maintenance purposes. The problem is that they can be discovered and exploited by other knowledgeable individuals. Some of the great hacker and virus stories started that way. So design integrity is a key issue.

Developing design integrity is primarily a technical issue and beyond the scope of this book. There are texts, courses, and periodicals on the subject, aimed primarily at the technician. It's a good discussion to have with your vendors, designers, programmers, MIS director, and security specialists, if you have them.

Encryption

Encryption is a technique that serves two purposes: access control and integrity. Simply defined, encryption transforms information through a rigorous but generally available process called an algorithm by using a unique and secret code or key. The key is a frequently changed string of characters that is combined in a complex mathematical fashion with the text of your message (clear text) by the algorithm. The result is unintelligible to all but those who possess the algorithm and key to retransform or decrypt it (see Figure 9-1).

Encryption can range from simple toys to supercomputer-class methodologies. Encryption requires an appropriate key to make information intelligible, so by controlling the key, you control access.

Figure 9–1. The encryption process.

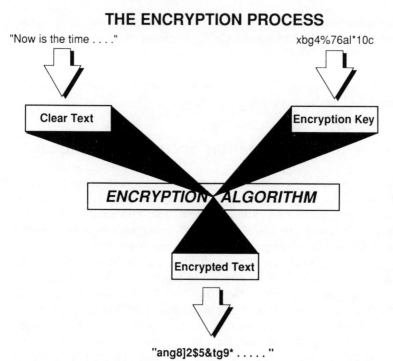

THE ENCRYPTION PROCESS

"Now is the time . . . ."   xbg4%76al*10c

Clear Text   **Encryption Key**

ENCRYPTION ALGORITHM

Encrypted Text

"ang8]2$5&tg9* . . . . . "

Using the encryption algorithm, clear text is combined with the encryption key, producing
encrypted text. To decrypt, using the same algorithm and key, the encrypted text is entered
and the clear text results.

If someone taps a communications line or gains access to an encrypted
file, he or she still needs the key and the same type of encryption
program or device you have used.

There are integrity features to encryption as well (see Figure 9-
2). Most current encryption schemes work in such a fashion that each
letter in the message is not only encoded itself but becomes part of
the encoding process of the rest of the message. Change one letter
in the encoded message and the entire message becomes untranslat-
able, even with the appropriate key. This is a great advantage in
authenticating messages. Is what I've got what you sent? Any effort
to modify the message, in effect, destroys the message. So if you can
translate it, it's authentic. The one major exception is the case in
which someone else besides the sender and receiver has the same

Figure 9-2. The integrity feature of the encryption process.

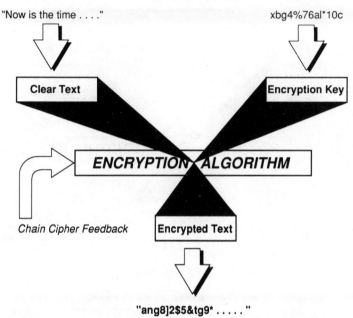

THE ENCRYPTION PROCESS
Integrity Feature

"Now is the time . . . ."   xbg4%76al*10c

Clear Text   Encryption Key

ENCRYPTION ALGORITHM

Chain Cipher Feedback   Encrypted Text

"ang8]2$5&tg9* . . . . . "

As each encrypted character is developed, it is fed back and combined with succeeding characters from the key and the clear text. As a result, if anyone attemps to alter any part of the message, the whole message becomes lost.

key. If that person decrypts, modifies, and reencrypts the message using the same key you have, it's the same as if a new message were being sent. There are ways to deal with this issue as well.

Electronic envelopes and signatures are applications of encryption (see Figure 9-3). Instead of encrypting the message itself, an electronic envelope is developed by passing the message through an encryption process and creating an encrypted appendage to go along with the message. The message is still in the clear. This is the same principle as hash totals in accounting, where you add, subtract, multiply, or divide all the items and append the result to a report. Any change to any of the fields and the hash total will no longer match.

Electronic envelopes are useful when you may not be interested in controlling disclosure of the message. You don't care who sees it,

Figure 9–3. Electronic envelopes.

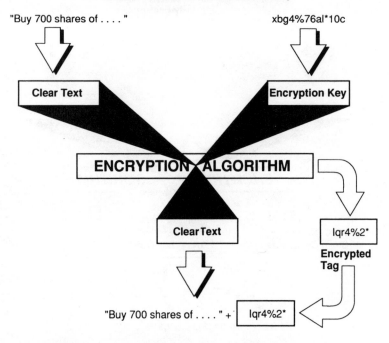

ELECTRONIC ENVELOPES

The clear text itself is not encrypted but is used with the encryption key to create an encrypted tag. The same process is performed at the receiving location and the tags are compared to verify message integrity.

you just don't want it modified. In that case, you don't have to incur all the intervening costs of encrypted transmission. All you need is authentication at the sending and receiving locations. In short, it's cheaper and easier to do.

A further variant on this principle is an electronic signature that encrypts the sender's identification, time of day sent, workstation ID, and other sender indicative information and appends it to the message. This authenticates the sender, not the message.

You can do one, two, or all of the above techniques. Many banks and financial services use message and electronic signature authentication extensively without actually encrypting the message. Some military applications require all three.

Encryption is available in hardware, software, and combination forms. There are several algorithms in use, the most popular being the DES (Data Encryption Standard) and the public key technique. Typically, DES encryption is used between a single sender and receiver. Even though the message may go through a whole series of intermediate points before getting to its final destination, it is usually intelligible only to the end points. Since both end points share a common key, transmission can be either way. There are DES techniques that can share the same key among many users, but the more users who share a key, the weaker the protection.

Public key encryption is different. It is built around the concept of many entry points transmitting to a single receiver (not unlike a bank night depository where many people can deposit funds but only a bank official can withdraw them). It can also allow a single entry point to broadcast to many receivers, all of whom share a common key. The difference is that in each case, unlike DES, the encrypted transmission is only one way. The same key *cannot* be used to go in the other direction. There are a number of situations in which one-way encryption is useful, most of them involving a large public user base and a single service point.

There are also other security techniques such as antivirus software, biometric identification, smart cards, and identification tokens.

10

Elements of a Continuity Program

What's in this chapter?

- Processing Facilities vs. Business Function
- The Business Function Approach
  —Business Impact Analysis
  —Strategies
  —Business Function Plans
- Disruption Threats and How to Deal With Them
- What's in a Continuity Plan?

In this book I define **continuity** as preventing, mitigating, and recovering from disruption. There are also other terms in use such as *contingency planning* and *disaster recovery*. There are several approaches to dealing with disruption as well.

Processing Facilities vs. Business Function

The two most common approaches can be described somewhat simplistically as the processing facilities approach and the business function approach.

The processing facilities approach is the more common, and it concentrates attention on ensuring that the processing center and its associated **information resources** are available and appropriately backed up. This view has its history in the centralized data center, which, as a focal point of service, has an obligation to ensure, within practical economic limits, continued support for its clients.

The business function approach is more global and takes cognizance of the fact that more and more information processing is done within the business unit itself. The key difference, however, is that it is a business-, not technology-, driven approach to continuity. In many cases, it encompasses all the concerns addressed in the processing facilities approach, but it does so as they relate to the business functions under consideration.

The business functions concerned are usually **information**-dependent. However, some enterprises have taken the concept to its logical conclusion and applied it to all critical business operations, regardless of information content. *The remainder of this discussion focuses on information-dependent operations.*

With the business function approach, *all* potential sources of disruption are taken into account, not just computers, software, and infrastructure, which are the primary concerns of the processing facilities view.

Which one is right? Both, depending on the viewpoint and specific objectives to be carried out. At some point, regardless of approach, the continued viability of the information processing center or centers must be addressed. However, the business function approach, I believe, is more valuable to the overall enterprise because it addresses the entire range of events and issues that could disrupt your critical business operations regardless of whether they relate to software and computers or the loss of key personnel.

The Business Function Approach

To get a better feeling for the business function approach, take a look at Figure 10-1. The process begins at the triangle's base with business impact analysis. It is very important that you understand what this process is and is not. It is not the risk and vulnerability assessment described in Chapter 4. This is something else.

Business Impact Analysis

Business impact analysis (BIA) is designed to first describe and prioritize the critical business functions within the enterprise and the critical information-related **applications** that support those business functions. Not all applications used by a critical business function are themselves critical. There may also be applications outside the business function

Figure 10-1. The business function approach.

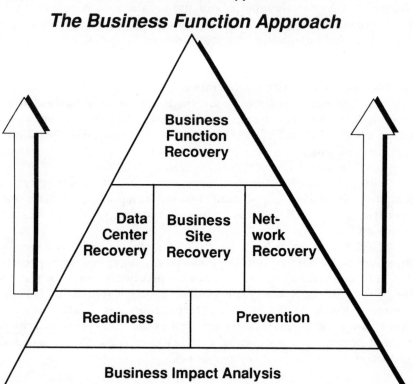

The process begins at the bottom of the triangle. The Business Impact Analysis lays the groundwork for the Readiness & Prevention Strategies. These, in turn, form the basis for the Datacenter, Business Site & Network Recovery Plans. Finally, these are coordinated into one Business Function Recovery Plan.

upon which the function depends. These are not intuitively obvious, nor are they always easy to get a consensus on. The designation of criticality sounds like a hard-nosed, numbers-driven, logical process, but don't you believe it. All managers like to think that their organizations are at the center of the business universe. Some, of course, would have a tough time proving it, but there is enough personal judgment, influence, and bias that go into these decisions to make them a fascinating exercise in corporate culture.

BIA's second objective is to determine how long the enterprise can do without the critical business functions or applications under consideration. You are not yet addressing specific threats, their likelihood, or their impact. You are coming from the opposite direction and asking, "How long can I tolerate a loss, for whatever reason, of this particular set of functions and applications?" In some cases, the answer may be minutes. In others, days. In still others, you may decide that an extended period is tolerable and what you thought was a critical application may not be.

The reasons for doing this are (1) to establish priority for continuity activities and (2) to establish some sort of value envelope in which to measure what preventive and **recovery** steps and associated expenses are warranted. Try your best to monetarize the statement of impact. If you can't handle your receivables for fifteen days, what does it cost in lost cash flow, cost of money, and recovery backlog management? Is there a ripple effect in other areas such as raw materials purchasing, payroll, or debt limits? What happens if receivables are out for two months? Where are the critical crossover points from inconvenient to serious to catastrophic? Are the intervals between those impacts days or hours?

The interesting thing about this approach is the new and valuable perspective it can give you about your enterprise. Usually some management assumptions are shattered during these exercises and some new insights are gained, not just about protecting information but about running the business as well. You will certainly gain greater insight into how and where your business information is used.

Notice that this part of the process requires much more business judgment than technical knowledge.

After you have identified and prioritized your target areas of concern in terms of not only the business functions and applications but also the processing functions that support them, you enter the next phase of assessing threats and vulnerabilities.

Strategies

If you have a strong feeling that, from a business standpoint, your receivables process is in the critical category, your next analysis addresses likely threats and how to deal with them. This is the next level in the triangle—the strategy level. Is the nature of the criticality and potential threats such that you can't rely strictly on a backup strategy? Must you dedicate more of your time and resources to a preventive strategy? The choices here are dictated not only by the critical nature of the process but also by the technology, staffing, management, administration, and infrastructure associated with the process. The odds are pretty good that a backup strategy would suffice for most accounts receivables situations.

But suppose you are running a mail-order business or airline reservation system. Then an outage, even a short one, may cost you irretrievable business losses. While you are out of action, passengers go to different airlines or customers lose the impulse to buy or go elsewhere and probably won't be back. If this is the case, you may wish to put more of your protective investment, still based on the conclusions of the business impact analysis, into a preventive strategy by dividing your network over several carriers, having two or more processing centers, redundant processes, and so forth. Here the objective is to stay on the air, not to recover after failure.

I'm discussing these two strategies as if they were separate and distinct. Actually, most organizations adopt a hybrid, creating a medley of preventive and recovery measures based on the circumstances.

Business Function Plans

The next level of continuity planning breaks the plan into three separate but related areas. For each critical business function, you must think in terms of each of these aspects:

1. *The data center (or processing center).* Don't take the term *data center* literally. I'm talking about your computing capability—software, staff, and all the support activities and equipment. That could be a miniprocessor stuck in a corner or a half mile of mainframes. It could also be a microprocessor.

Would you go through an elaborate planning program for a microprocessor-based business function? Probably not, if it was one micro. Your major concerns probably lie in backing up data, having original software copies on hand, and having an alternative machine. But string a group of those machines together in a local area network (LAN) or simply put them all in one place, unconnected, and develop a flood, and you may have a major continuity issue on your hands. The point is, don't judge the need for continuity planning by the processing **platform.** Judge it by the business function.

2. *Communications.* This may be a LAN. It may be a dedicated data network. It may be a voice network or all of the above. How

much of this do you control, and how much of it is in the hands of the common carriers? How many carriers do you have? Who installs and maintains your LAN cabling and network management?

Take special notice of your voice network (which may also be your fax network). In some organizations, losing one or both can have a much more devastating effect than losing the computers. Try running your mail-order business or airline without voice facilities.

Your network strategy may also be different from your processing center strategy. Can you back up an entire net? Should you install bypass facilities to keep yourself going? Can you switch from dedicated to dial-up lines and use the public network or networks to keep you going? Are there service level guarantees from the carriers that you want to avail yourself of?

3. *The "office."* Here I refer to the operational and administrative elements that form the business structure around the information process. During power blackouts and fires, there have been examples of data centers that have remained physically operational through backup power but could not be staffed because people were not being permitted in the building or couldn't get to the center because of lack of elevator access. What happens in a crippling snowstorm or hurricane? The **systems** and applications may survive, but the operator, supervisor, and data-entry personnel may be stuck miles away.

The question of key personnel comes into play here as well. Do you have critical people who, if they left, became seriously ill, or died, would take the only available knowledge of how the system and applications ran with them? It's not uncommon. It also isn't uncommon for application documentation to be poor, incomplete, or hopelessly out of date. These are continuity issues that are as serious as a fire or flood.

Going beyond the direct information handling, are there other departmental functions that, if curtailed, say, because of strike or bomb scare, could cripple your operation?

Each of these three aspects can be assessed and developed separately, but ultimately they need to be put together to provide a seamless continuity plan for the business function. These business function plans, in turn, need to be blended into an enterprise business recovery plan.

Notice that all through this process, the dominant theme is business considerations, not technology. That characteristic is probably the single most important point of departure that this approach has with other types of contingency plans. But if you consider how information processing has become integrated with the business process at the user, department, division, and enterprise levels, I believe it is the most appropriate approach for today's environment.

Disruption Threats and How to Deal With Them

I divide disruption threats into two major categories: (1) physical and (2) logical (i.e., nonphysical).

The physical threats are pretty obvious:

- Fire
- Water—rising
- Water—falling
  (the damage and defense are different in each case)
- Wind and storm
- Snow, sleet, and ice
- Earthquakes and mudslides
- Willful damage or threat of damage
- Explosion
- Structural failure
- Toxic substance release
- Loss of personnel—strike, transportation failure, etc.
- Power loss
- HVAC (Heating, Ventilation, Air Conditioning) loss
- Communications loss
- Other infrastructural failure
- Physical equipment failure
- Others, ranging from hordes of locusts to killer fogs

Communications failure can be induced by physical or logical problems. The construction equipment industry vehemently denies it but all of us in the protection business swear that there is a highly sophisticated piece of hardware in common use known as the "cable-seeking backhoe." This unit of machinery, with uncanny accuracy and unrelenting singlemindedness, zeroes in on any communications or power cable buried anywhere in the general vicinity of the construction project in progress and tears it up, cutting it in the least accessible location and in the least reparable way. I've seen too many of these incidents to believe it is all accidental. There is a cosmic conspiracy at work here and it could be after you.

Physical disruption was everyone's major worry—until recently. Clearly, it is still a major issue; replacing a burned or flooded data center is not a trivial exercise. However, some of the most recent and comprehensive communications failures have been logically induced, primarily by software failure, operator error, and, occasionally, poor equipment design. Logically induced outages are no longer regarded as relatively minor glitches with containable impacts and short recovery cycles.

The "mean time to pain" (i.e., how long it takes for negative effects to be felt) has been reduced to hours and minutes rather than days and weeks. If you are dependent on automated systems and applications for running your entire business and not just back-room reporting and accounting, the time between "failure and feeling it" is bound to get shorter. As it does, those threats that may have once belonged to the quick-fix category become more important. If you can no longer tolerate being out of action for even short periods of time, such events become increasingly important in continuity planning.

Another reason for the increased attention to logically induced outages is interconnection and interoperability. If a software glitch is restricted to a single processor, the impact may be significant but containable. If that same glitch spreads through a network to a number of processors, the impact can become geometric. An AT&T 800-number outage in 1990 was the result of a poorly deployed software change that affected just about every programmable switch in the system. The result was a major loss of service, which impacted confidence and business, at least temporarily. I remember hearing a network specialist say, perhaps with some hyperbole, that the switches were physically designed to take and be protected from a direct hit from a nuclear weapon. "But," he said, "take one lousy piece of software and. . . ."

Perhaps the most compelling example of the logically induced outage is the virus. Large networks and collections of processors have been taken out not just once but repeatedly by software attacks.

The obvious point is that there are classes of software and operational errors and attacks that, while not as final as the destruction of a building, can still be highly damaging and perhaps lethal.

Any continuity plan designed for the 1990s has to take both classes into account. A continuity plan is a dynamic document that should be reviewed and tested at least annually and whenever a trigger event, such as new hardware, software, or applications, or change of location or organization, takes place. Anything that changes the continuity context should trigger a review and, if necessary, a retest of the continuity plan. If the plan isn't tested, and if the test doesn't reflect current conditions, you can't claim that it's effective.

What's in a Continuity Plan?

An effective continuity plan should address the following:

1. *Scope of coverage.* Is this a data-center-only plan? Are communications and office site included? Are business functions, applications, locations, and departments included?

2. *Objectives.* What is the plan designed to do? Restore the entire service in the face of total disaster? Respond to partial outages as well? Respond to outages by providing partial, reduced service or total service? Provide interim processing capabilities until new facilities can be provided? Failure to state objectives will result in misunderstandings and misdirected expectations.

3. *Strategy.* Prevention steps and recovery steps.

4. *Threats and countermeasures.* Physical and logical disruptions.

5. *File and software backup storage procedures, sites, and responsibilities.* Are you going to store your backup data off site? If so, where? This is not the same as having a backup processing center. Do not ignore backup processes and facilities for your LANs and PCs, including portables. Emphasize the information, not the technology.

6. *Processing site backup facilities.* Some argue that backup sites should, by definition, be a significant distance away from the main storage site. The extent of this separation can range from the impact area of a nuclear hit to the boundaries of common weather or geological centers and power grids. There is certainly some logic to this approach, but there are counterbalancing concerns as well. For example:

- *Travel time, cost, and logistics.* I know of one situation that required obtaining backup tapes from an extremely remote site during

a major snowstorm. The vehicle and driver sent to retrieve the tapes never made it.
- *Management.* The more remote a facility, the more difficult it is to manage and administer. You're supposed to be sending backups to this facility with some regularity. If the transfer is being made physically, as opposed to by transmission, you have major logistical and transportation concerns to deal with.
- *Threat priority.* Plan the backup strategy to fit the primary threats you're concerned about. If your principal concerns are such things as infrastructure failure, fire, logical failure, and other site- rather than region-related problems, then stay within the region. If hurricanes, earthquakes, or war-zone issues are primary, then choose a site that's a reasonable distance outside the regional perimeter.

There are several options when it comes to backup sites:

- *Cold site.* A space with basic facilities such as water and light but not much else. The least expensive alternative, but also the least responsive.
- *Warm site.* Space plus expanded facilities, usually including some computing hardware and telecommunications. You may also store your backup files here. Some transition and preparation is necessary to get off the ground. You may need to bring additional hardware and software to the site.
- *Hot site.* This can cover a range of possibilities. On the one end are fully operational centers with resident staff running in parallel with the primary site and capable of cutting over within seconds to provide essentially seamless support. There are other less elaborate but nonetheless responsive units that have resident copies of current software and data but are not keeping up with the transaction flow. These can be brought on-line in a very short time, but not instantaneously. Clearly these are the most expensive alternatives and should be considered only for those applications that must stay up nonstop.

7. *Backup processing site arrangements.* There are a number of them:

- Buy your own hardware and software and staff it yourself.

- Subscribe to one of the many backup services. These can vary widely in cost; contract terms; available hardware, software, and support; allowances for plan tests; and priorities in case of multiple user demand. If a power outage hits a major metropolitan area, all of the service's clients may try to get on the backup system at the same time. Check the terms of your contract and the costs very carefully, or use a disinterested consultant to help you. These services are ethical, but their offerings, terms, and conditions are complex. Be sure you know what you are getting for your money. Equally important, know what you're not getting.
- Enter into mutual support agreements with other organizations. I've included this option here for completeness. I seldom, if ever, recommend it. The odds are stacked heavily against your getting what you need from another enterprise that may be in the same boat you are. No matter how the terms of the agreement are stated, enforcing it is nearly impossible. I have heard of two organizations signing a mutual support agreement with close to 90 percent utilization on both systems. How could you possibly expect one to spare the time to back up the other? It sounds attractive, but it seldom works, even within the same organization.

Remember that in addition to processing facilities, you need to accommodate people with workspaces, telephones, food, and other amenities, perhaps for a long while.

8. *Telecommunications.* If a backup site is going to support a network, you need the communications facilities. This could be the biggest expenditure and most important item on your backup list.

9. *Staffing and management responsibilities.* Who does what? There is an important issue here that is often overlooked. In staffing a continuity plan, remember the circumstances under which you will be operating. You are not going from Site A to Site B, period, unless Site A is a total loss. Typically, you will go to Site B and at the same time you will be working to bring Site A back up. You are not planning a permanent migration, just a temporary stay. Do you have enough trained staff and management to run two sites at the same time, especially at a distance? Many plans fail for lack of available trained staff.

10. *Contact, transfer, and deployment plan.* This includes a list of telephone numbers and call responsibilities. How will transportation be supplied? Do you have twenty-four-hour hot-line travel service? How will you establish living arrangements, provide child care, if necessary, and deal with medical restrictions and disabilities? How will the people be paid? Are there union restrictions to contend with?

11. *Supplies and infrastructure.* Don't forget the basics such as pencils and adhesive tape and the speciality items such as check stock or report forms.

12. *Budgets and cost estimates.*

13. *A test plan.* The vast majority of continuity, contingency, or disaster recovery plans in existence have not been adequately tested, if they've been tested at all. If you're not going to test your plan in a comprehensive and realistic manner, you have dramatically reduced its usefulness and, worse yet, you have probably created a false sense of security with top management. Tests can be expensive, disruptive, often embarrassing, and difficult. They are also necessary.

14. *A plan maintenance program.* Plans are dynamic and need to be reviewed, updated, and retested on either a time or event scale. The interval should probably be at least yearly for any complex plan. For an organization whose systems are undergoing constant change, a major event such as hardware, software, or application changes is probably a better trigger than the mere passage of time. Items 13 and 14 can often make the difference between a reliable, practical plan and a document that gathers dust on a shelf.

Continuity planning is an area where getting outside help may be an intelligent and cost-effective move. There are many organizations, including my employer, that provide these services. We believe in tailor-made plans. There are also a number of organizations that provide ready-made plans. They cost less and are better than nothing, but unless the resulting continuity plan really reflects your situation, it can be counterproductive.

11

Managing an Ongoing Program

What's in this chapter?

- Functions Needed to Run an IP Program
  —Overall Risk Assessment
  —Overall Risk Management
  —Strategies, Plans, and Budgets
  —Policies, Standards, and Procedures
  —Classification
  —Enforcement and Incident Reporting
  —Technical IP Management
  —Training and Awareness
  —Quality Control
- The IP Organization
  —Reporting Structure

Defining, developing, and initially deploying an **information protection** (IP) program are enough to keep any manager occupied for a while. However, IP is a process, not an event. Therefore, the process has to be managed, reviewed, updated, and improved. This chapter looks at the management aspects of an IP program once it has been put in place.

Functions Needed to Run an IP Program

Notice that I refer to *functions*, not departments, not managers, not staffs. How you implement and deploy these functions is subject to a number of variables, not the least of which are the scope of the program and your available resources. What I'm defining here are the bases. How you cover them is your call and will vary widely with circumstances and needs.

Overall Risk Assessment

Overall **risk assessment** includes:

- **Information resource** (asset) valuation
- Impact analysis of loss or compromise
- Risk assessment (potential threats and probability)
- Vulnerability analysis

These are not constant processes, but they are not one-time events either. The results of initial risk assessment efforts should be periodically reviewed and updated to reflect changing conditions. If you have the right chemistry and available management resources, this is a candidate for task force or committee review.

Overall Risk Management

Overall **risk management** is a standing requirement, and it is fundamentally a management task, although staff support can greatly assist. This can range from several full-time people to one part-time person. The action options are:

- Risk prevention—reduce the chance of occurrence
- Risk containment—limit the effects of an occurrence
- Insurance—transfer the financial impact of the occurrence
- Self-insurance—internal provision for the financial impact
- Do nothing—accept the risk as is

The last option is not only viable, it may also be the best alternative, at least for the moment. For example, if future plans call for construction of a major new building that will incorporate in its design many of your physical and environmental protection requirements, then for the moment, it may be most prudent to continue to live with the issue. The important point is: *This should be a conscious and agreed-upon management decision, not the result of inaction or inattention.*

You need an analysis process (nothing elaborate) that takes all of the risks identified during risk assessment and puts them in one or more of the action (or inaction) option categories listed above. Then you need agreement from appropriate management. This may not prevent the roof from falling in on your head if there is a major blowup, but it should help, and it will help keep the auditors off your back.

Strategies, Plans, and Budgets

The strategies, plans, and budgets covered here are the recurring variety. They should be developed by chronology and by function:

• *The chronological view.* For fiscal year 199X, what are the IP programs that will be in place? What new ones will be launched? What will be discontinued or modified? What are the staffing requirements, capital requirements, and operating overhead requirements to make this happen? What are the costs? How will they be apportioned? How will they be approved?

• *The functional view.* This approach simply takes a different cut at the same questions, stretching each IP functional area out to whatever the planning horizon is in your organization and projecting year-by-year activities and costs.

Obviously, both of these approaches should be integrated into whatever planning and budget procedures you already have in place. It's important that they don't get lost, however. You should be able to identify major IP processes and expenses within your plans and budgets. This will not encompass all costs, since there are many lower-level IP measures that are covered by the general cost of doing business.

It will probably come as no surprise to you that most enterprises really don't have a good grasp of what they are spending or should be spending on IP. The percentages of 3–4 percent that I cited earlier resulted primarily from estimates, not actual accounting figures.

The costs of dedicated staff and departments, specialized software and devices, and, perhaps, some major procedures are reasonably easy to identify. But you are also trying to create a state of mind and a mode of doing business, strongly akin to a safety or quality program. You won't be able to do more than estimate (with less than perfect accuracy) what the entire program costs. You probably won't be able to identify the monetary value of the resulting protection with great precision either.

Policies, Standards, and Procedures

Policies, standards, and procedures are necessary to give comprehensive, consistent, effective, and efficient guidance throughout your organization (see Chapter 12). You will not only need to establish these but from time to time create, update, revise, and perhaps eliminate them. This means that someone needs to be responsible for the process.

Don't try to make your IP policies, standards, and procedures different *in form* from the rest of the enterprise's program unless, of course, there is no program. However, do not shortchange the *content* of your policies, standards, and procedures simply because other subject areas are poorly or incompletely covered.

How you publish, promulgate, get feedback on, and manage the process is almost as important as the content you publish. Just between the two of us, how often do you go to the corporate standards manual? Is there a corporate standards manual? How often is it updated? Do you keep your copy updated? What's your opinion of its effectiveness? What's the general opinion of its effectiveness? Don't expect any greater degree of attention to IP than any other subject in those manuals.

If you want to get attention paid to IP, you're going to have to take additional steps such as awareness programs, special publications, and probably, most important, just keep bringing it up (appropriately) until it becomes a matter of standard operating procedure. The objective is for everyone to become his or her own IP officer. That state takes a while and some effort to develop.

By all means, develop policies, standards, and procedures for IP. Just remember that policies, standards, and procedures don't run an enterprise, people do. We judge people by what they do as well as what they say. The same holds true for organizations. The courts have been known to throw out policy manuals as indicators of corporate direction if it can be shown that common practice ran contrary to those policies. You have to *do* it as well as *say* it.

Classification

After establishing a classification structure (see Chapter 3), you need an ongoing classification process and some way of checking to see whether it's being done completely and correctly. The classification itself is the responsibility of the information owners. The checkup can done by internal audit, data security, and continuity administration if they exist, or on a peer- or self-review basis. Like policies, standards, and procedures, of which they are usually a part, the rules of classification, especially if they are involved and difficult to use, may gather dust at a rapid rate. Write them to be used—and use them—in a practical, common-sense way.

Enforcement and Incident Reporting

This is an area where judgment and a sense of proportion are necessary. Clearly, you don't want to start a reign of terror, but one of the primary dogmas of management is, "Don't expect what you don't inspect."

There may be an understandable tendency to leave these types of activities to the specialists—internal audit, IP administrators, legal and general security, if you have any of these functions. If an incident that is significant in its consequences does arise, by all means, involve the professionals. This is especially true if it seems likely that criminal prosecution is going to take place. It's very easy to taint evidence or violate an individual's civil and legal rights while playing police officer.

On the other hand, it is very important for the success of the program that all employees understand that management means what it says. This involves not just delivering the message but enforcing it as well. If you are the manager responsible for the department, division, or enterprise, you should be identified with the enforcement program.

When it comes to incident reporting, there should be a clear process available to all employees to report, without prejudice, any violation they encounter, *including by their own management.* This means both professional and management involvement. Unless the possible outcome suggests otherwise, such as potential escape of a criminal, the individual being cited should be notified in a complete and timely way and given full opportunity to respond.

Your personnel should be encouraged to point out procedural miscues directly to the individual first; then to local management. If the magnitude of the problem is sufficient to warrant disciplinary action and it's clear that the action is deliberate and malicious, then the employee observing the activity should go straight to management.

This is a tough process to get started and maintain in many organizations, for all the reasons you might imagine. Nobody likes a squealer or a bounty hunter. Nevertheless, unless you take the treatment of violations seriously and make it known that you are taking it seriously, your **security** program will be missing a major part of its effectiveness.

Think this one through thoroughly and assign the functional responsibilities carefully. Try a dry run; test it out with human resources, legal, and the management information systems (MIS) organization, if they exist.

Most important, don't threaten what you don't plan to deliver. If you represent the enterprise as ready to demote, dismiss, or even prosecute individuals for IP violations and you know that the entire corporate culture runs against it, don't make those threats. Your people will see through it, and you'll be putting yourself and the enterprise in an untenable position. Don't conduct public floggings just to prove how serious you are. Use that most valuable of all management qualities—common sense.

Technical IP Management

These are the areas responsible for supporting the software and hardware features, design criteria, standards and procedures, and other technically based activities in support of IP. This includes managing the authorization, password control, and rules writing for access control facilities. It includes managing the **continuity** plans, backup sites, and physical access control systems such as key cards and monitors. It includes the oversight of the software selection, development, and maintenance processes to ensure that security and continuity specifications and requirements are met.

Where does technical IP management belong organizationally? Some people argue for total independence of these functions, and there is some validity to their claims. I have developed a healthy respect for and belief in the concepts of objectivity, arm's length, and separation of duties. But these concepts are not absolutes.

If you can't achieve perfect objectivity, at least achieve operational effectiveness. There is also a downside to arm's length, and it usually is best described as ending up "out of the loop." You can't influence what you can't see.

If the control functions are going to be organizationally separated from the actual development and operations activities, then they should be placed where they can still exercise leverage on the process. If they are contained within the development and operations functions, they should have sufficient clout and access to higher management to be effective. Don't develop these functions just to look good on an organizational chart.

Training and Awareness

There is a difference between training and awareness (see Chapter 15). Awareness creates a general level of understanding and motivation to protect information resources. Training is more how-to in its orientation and may be highly specialized by subject or audience.

Obviously, programs of this type don't just happen. They need to be planned, designed, and staffed; materials must be developed, tested, scheduled, presented, evaluated, and modified. Curriculum and course content need to be specified. Will you present IP as a single program? Security alone? Continuity alone? Do you need a special class on writing access control rules? A special session for administrative staff on handling classified hard-copy materials?

Target audiences should be described. What will you tell senior management? What do you tell new employees? Do you combine technicians, users, and administrative staff in the same sessions? How often do you run them? Where? Who presents what? What media do you want to use? Do you use outside sources? To do what?

If you have a central training group, you might consider IP as one more subject area for their curricula. They can provide general administration; you and your protection specialists can contribute content and instructors. Don't turn the actual instruction over to the educators entirely. This is a management and motivation issue, and it requires management participation.

The opposite approach is to use the training group as a resource and run your own program. This, I think, is preferable for the first round. The folks who developed, approved, and are implementing the protection program—especially local management—should be deeply involved in presenting and promoting it.

If you don't have a training group, the solution is simple but not all that palatable. It puts yet another responsibility on your plate. By all means seek to delegate the mechanics to members of your (or somebody else's) staff. Don't try to delegate the responsibility, and do be an active participant.

Quality Control

You can look at quality control at least two ways, and both of them are valid for IP:

1. *Control of the quality of the actual information, software, hardware, and other information resources.* This covers development, operations, and end usage. This is often referred to as quality assurance (QA).

2. *Quality of the IP process.* Is it performing up to expectations? Although internal and external audit may be active in this area, they are usually spread so thin that the best you can expect is partial and sporadic coverage of the program. If, after all the time and energy you've put into this thing, you want to determine whether it has been effective, you probably need a more directed and concentrated review process. You may want to consider outside consultants for this service.

Quality assurance is a function that is often confused with information protection. The principal attributes that distinguish QA from IP are efficiency and effectiveness.

QA is closely related to IP. QA's major purpose is to see that the information process operates in the way and to the degree management desires. QA is pretty common in software development, but it should actually encompass the entire information process. In my opinion, many administrative functions could use more QA attention. Similar to the manufacturing quality control process, there are two basic ways of carrying it out:

1. Reactive processes, such as test and review.
2. Proactive processes, such as design specs, design and production interlocks, incentive programs, quality groups, and the like.

In the ideal situation, IP considerations should be part of the overall QA process. What does management expect for IP? In what way and to what degree? Whether management's expectations are appropriate and within the realm of good practice is a separate set of issues. These are often pursued by audit.

The major selling point for integrating IP quality issues under the QA function is that they will then come up in the context of the other objectives, specs, and constraints associated with the development or operating process under consideration. Some security and continuity specialists feel that this is a formula for losing every battle. They feel that the other considerations will always be given priority. My feeling is that if IP has that low a priority in development or operating management's estimation, it's going to lose under any arrangement.

If IP considerations are included during design walk-throughs, spec reviews, and test and deployment release, to name just a few decision points in software development, they stand a better chance of being implemented than if they come after the **system** or **application** is developed. Then you find yourself trying to retrofit onto hardened code, which is not easy and very expensive.

The IP Organization

I have deliberately left until last the question of how and whether you should create a distinct IP organization (or, alternatively, separate information security and continuity organizations). I think the functions of security and continuity should be highly correlated and cooperative, but whether they should be combined is an enterprise-by-enterprise call.

The first question is: Do you need a standing, distinct organization at all (understanding that the organization could range from a single person to a small army)? I have tried to distinguish *function* from *organization* throughout these discussions because organizational considerations tend to cloud and confuse the underlying issues involved. They are certainly important, but I believe you should get the required processes defined before you try to map them against the current organization or structure a new organization.

If you agree with me that most, if not all, of the functions I've previously described have a place in your enterprise, let's examine the pros and cons of three ways you can organize them:

1. *A separate organizational structure* with a corporate information protection administrator and counterpart departments or missions spread throughout the organization. These departments or missions usually report to local management, but take "functional guidance" from the corporate administrator. This is classic example of matrixed management. (To whom the corporate administrator reports is another issue.)

- *Pros.* Maximum visibility; clear functional definition within the corporate structure; dedicated activity, which, with all else being equal, will tend to produce a higher level of sustained protection; career recognition and potential growth paths; the opportunity

to attract experienced professionals; a clear sign both inside and outside the enterprise that IP is being taken seriously.
- *Cons.* Expense; for the size of your organization, it may be overkill; it may run counter to corporate culture; it may tend to create among other managers and employees a psychology that they have no IP responsibility, since the specialists are *totally responsible* for IP; improperly staffed and improperly managed, it can become yet another organizational backwater or leper colony; if too far separated from the information process, it may be "out of the loop"; it may be the source of internal conflict, although this may not always be a bad thing.

2. *No visible specialist organization.* Instead, the functions are integrated into existing job descriptions and the responsibilities for IP, including planning, budgeting, technical, procedural, training, enforcement, and quality control, are laid on line and staff management, as appropriate. This is the extreme case of everyone being his or her own security officer.

- *Pros.* Minimal expense; minimal disruption; minimum bureaucracy; it places maximum emphasis on the role of the owner, user, and service supplier to ensure that security and continuity are being carried out appropriately.
- *Cons.* It seldom works; effectiveness, consistency, and comprehensiveness are very difficult to achieve; other job pressures tend to deprioritize IP considerations; no focal point; it projects a low-priority image to employees, customers, vendors, regulators, the public, and the press; it looks like no protection.

3. *Hybrid.* An almost infinite variety of options between the two extremes. My preference is to start with Option 1 and determine the irreducible minimum of additional staff and organization required to carry out your functional objectives for IP. Move the pointer up a few spaces and examine whether an expansion of the organization would provide functional improvements and still be cost-effective and culturally acceptable. You may also wish to phase this process—year one organization, year two etc.

Clearly, all of this is predicated on several premises:

• That the enterprise is within your purview. If all you're worried about or can reasonably expect to influence is your own division or department, then a greatly scaled-down organizational decision is before you. Do you need someone full-time or with a primary job designation to handle your IP needs?

• That you have sufficient information processing traffic and dependence on information resources to warrant a full-scale program.

• That you have sufficiently valuable information resources and sufficiently apparent threats and motivation to warrant a full-scale program.

Reporting Structure

Reporting structure is always tricky. DeMaio's first law of IP organization is: *Put it where it has the best chance to survive and successfully carry out its mission.* It's dangerous and runs against classical management dogma to organize around a person, but in the early stages of development, there is a lot to be said for placing the fledgling organization with the management that gave it life.

Placing an IP department or departments in line operations that own critical resources, with MIS, or with the controller (or provost in a university) are, in my mind, the best alternatives. Placing it under staff functions such as administration, legal, or even human resources can be viable but depends on the quality, reputation, influence, and mind-set of those units.

However, even if the program was sponsored and first saw life there, I do not believe IP should ever report to internal audit. Internal audit typically sees its function as review and assessment. And although these processes are part of the IP function, they are only part. Most internal audit units disavow, properly, a responsibility for development, planning, technical support, and so on.

Some enterprises separate and place IP *assessment* in the hands of internal audit. I have less objection to that, as long as it can provide adequate coverage with all of its other responsibilities. This usually falls to the electronic data processing (EDP) auditors within internal audit, if they exist.

One last word: Please don't let the organizational tail wag the IP dog. Organization is a primary issue, no doubt, but get the goals, objectives, functional requirements, and characteristics of the overall program described and agreed upon before tackling organization. Otherwise, you may not like the results.

12

Minimizing Bureaucracy

In making it this far along in understanding **information protection** (IP), I suspect that some of you may have arrived at the conclusion that IP could become a bureaucrat's paradise. You're right. Like most control-oriented processes, IP could become intensely bureaucratic in the wrong hands and with poorly thought-out goals, objectives, and attitudes. But it need not be. That's the point of this chapter.

There is no escaping the fact that you will be introducing a new administrative and technical process into the enterprise or some part of it and, as a result, restricting some people's freedom of operation. These two items alone will not do much for the program's or your own popularity index.

Also, bureaucracy is in the eye of the beholder: The procedure I'm recommending to you, in true team-player spirit, is a major breakthrough in productivity, efficiency, and good management. The procedure you're arrogantly imposing on me is a step backward into the dark ages of bureaucratic waste and inefficiency. (It's probably the same procedure.) That's why early manager and user "buy-in" is so important. A sense of authorship and proprietorship among those who must implement the program can do a great deal to defuse the bureaucratic image.

But even if you can't make the image go away completely, you can still take major steps to streamline the reality. Besides the fundamental mind-set of the individuals involved, which may be cured only by a major housecleaning, the two mainstays of bureaucratic pettifoggery are:

1. Organizational overkill (why use one department when twelve will do?), turf wars, and organization chart roulette.
2. Procedural overkill (how to micromanage a program into paralysis).

This chapter concentrates on policies, standards, procedures, guidelines, mission statements, and job descriptions—defining and differentiating each one, exploring their characteristics and implications, outlining their use and misuse, and providing criteria for choosing the right vehicle and avoiding a bureaucratic nightmare.

Differentiating Policies, Standards, Procedures, and Guidelines

What is a policy? Oddly enough, there is a lot of room for disagreement here. I have seen policy manuals that take up yards of space on bookshelves; I have also seen policies cut into marble facades over doors. Although size itself doesn't define the policy, it gives a pretty good indicator about what the enterprise thinks it should be and do. A *policy* is a high-level statement of enterprise beliefs, goals, and objectives and the general means for their attainment for a specified subject area. Overblown policies happen when the *general means* become very specific and detailed means and the *specified area* (in this case, information protection) becomes far more detailed, covering subjects such as password management. I don't believe you can have a policy on password management. You can have a standard, guideline, or procedure, but not a policy.

A *standard* is a mandatory statement of design or implementation. It is also a norm for measurement and, as such, should be restricted to situations where performance to specific measurement is required. There need not be a standard for every subject covered by a policy. In fact, there shouldn't be. Standards are expensive to administer correctly, and if you don't plan to administer them fully and correctly, don't call them standards. Call them guidelines or procedures, or don't write them at all.

Procedures and *guidelines* are essentially how-to instructions that support some part of the policy or a standard. However, they may not have come into being directly as a result of a policy or standard; they may have existed first, and the standards and policies were formalized around them. Here's how I distinguish between procedures and guidelines (not everyone agrees with me on this): A procedure should be mandatory (with some mechanism for seeking a variance). Guidelines should allow for some level of local option and management interpretation.

I believe that the choice of vehicle below the policy level should start from the bottom up. If a guideline will do it for you, stop right there. I have a particular phobia about standards that aren't really standards.

IP Policies

Even if the policy is short and set at a high level, I believe every organization should have an IP policy.

Benefits of an IP Policy

In no order of priority and with no pretense that the list is all-inclusive, these are the benefits of having an IP policy:

- It helps the enterprise develop a prioritized value for **information.**
- It's an enabling platform for protection strategies, plans, and implementation.
- It provides a clear and consistent internal statement for management and employee guidance.
- Along with standards, guidelines, and procedures, it provides a yardstick for IP review and assessment.

- It provides a clear and consistent external statement for all interested parties (e.g., stockholders, customers, vendors, processing partners, regulators, auditors, the media, and the public).
- It contributes to the effectiveness and direction of overall enterprise **risk management.**
- Finally, it may assist in or be required for responding to legal and regulatory requirements.

Many enterprises get along with informal policies, passed along by word of mouth, custom, folklore, and the like. Why do you need an explicit, written IP policy? For these reasons:

- Information is different enough to warrant a specific, explicit statement. Put another way, information protection is not an intuitively obvious process; in fact, it runs counter to our basic instincts.
- There is a great deal of ethical ambiguity about information. If you don't believe me, find me someone who owns more than one VCR and has never copied a rental tape.
- There is great deal of legal and regulatory ambiguity—indeed, conflict. A short review of the laws affecting information in the United States alone will reveal a rather confused state. Add international requirements, and you can have a field day.
- An explicit policy may be mandated. For example, U.S. banking regulations require that all affected financial institutions have one.
- As a common base for management, an explicit policy is far superior to an implicit one, even if the explicit statement puts heavy reliance on individual management judgment.
- Only an explicit statement can be convincing in courts of law, customer contracts, vendor relations, acquisitions, and public relations.

Characteristics of a Good IP Policy

The characteristics of a good IP policy are not much different from those required of any policy. A good IP policy should:

1. *Be simple and understandable.* The language should be written to be understood by the least educated individuals required to abide

by the policy. Jargon and special organizational references should be minimized. Do not assume that all "knowledge workers" have extensive vocabularies or deep technical competence.

2. *Be applicable.* Applicability is especially important if you have been borrowing or researching the policies of other enterprises. Do the characteristics, requirements, and environments stated or implied in the policy actually describe your enterprise? If not, get them out of there. They could be the beginning of a whole chain of standards, guidelines, procedures, missions, job descriptions, software, and hardware acquisitions and processes that don't fit.

3. *Be feasible.* Can the average person do what you're asking? (This isn't the same as Item 1.) Suppose I ask someone to fly unaided off the top of a building. What I want is probably very clearly understood. The problem is, he can't. If the solution is left to the reader in too many cases or requires more effort, predisposition, or knowledge than you have a right to expect (or are paying for), then don't expect the policy to be carried out.

4. *Be enforceable.* This has a kinship with feasibility, but it has a slightly different spin. If you state or imply that certain activities will be subject to sanctions and punishment or that certain individuals are charged with enforcing the rules, make sure they can be enforced. Do you have enough people to monitor and enforce? Will you actually do what you say you'll do? Don't threaten dismissal if you know that human resources or a union will block you every time. (See also Item 6.)

5. *Be phased in.* Any new IP policy, if it addresses dates at all, should allow for gradual development of the desired situation and results. It should also facilitate revision and modification.

6. *Provide positive guidance, not prohibition and punishment.* I once challenged a consultant who was working with me to write an information security policy without using the negative. He did it, and without resorting to convoluted language or semantic tricks. An IP policy should not read like the Ten Commandments, the majority of which begin "Thou shalt not. . . ." I find a practically unbroken stream of prohibitions a disheartening form of behavioral guidance. You are not trying to entrap, threaten, intimidate, or even inhibit individuals in performing their legitimate activities. You are trying to assist them in performing them safely and with appropriate integrity. A high violation count is a sure sign that your program *isn't* working. "Gotcha" has no place in IP vocabulary and especially in a policy.

7. *Avoid "all or nothing" statements.* Words such as *ensure, absolute, total, complete, eliminate,* and *guarantee* are terms most organizations are reluctant to put in their contracts with others. Think twice about putting them in your IP policy. They set objectives that you may neither desire nor be able to meet. They could also be used against you in a contractual sense if you publish your policy externally and then fail to reach the stated objectives. You don't ever want to hear: "But, Mr. X, it states right here in your Information Protection policy that you intend to ensure total protection for all information assets developed by you or given over to your care and use. My client feels that by permitting a virus to affect your files, which contained my client's information, you have fallen far short of your fiduciary responsibilities and the goals and objectives you publicly proclaim in your policy document. Therefore we are seeking. . . ."

8. *Enable the concept of risk acceptance as well as risk avoidance.* This is related to, but slightly different from, Item 7. There are certain risks that prudent businesspeople and organizational administrators have to take. The alternative measures may be too costly, insufficiently effective, or flat-out impossible. Don't write a policy that speaks about eliminating risk. Use the words *reducing* or *mitigating.* Make sure you don't undermine the position of management by making the prudent acceptance of certain risks no longer acceptable.

9. *Cover information in all forms.* This is a judgment call. You may choose to cover information only in electronic, computer-based form. I have a very strong preference for covering all forms of information and information in all forms. My reasoning is: The asset is the information. Does the value or impact from misuse, corruption, destruction, or disclosure change when it passes from a hard disk to a printed document or a voice communication over telephone lines? I doubt it. The susceptibility to threat may change (often for the worse in nontechnology settings). The technology is a secondary form of **information resource,** worthy of protection in its own right, but it should not completely dominate the policy.

Frequently an IP policy gets written for "computerized information only" because the sponsoring department is management information systems (MIS). Computerized information is the limit of its responsibilities. If you are going to establish a limited program, make sure that it is carefully described and advertised as such. Don't create false expectations. Everyone, including you, should understand that you do not have a complete IP program.

10. *Be appropriate in the level of content and detail.* What difference does it make? Plenty, if you subscribe to the idea that policy can be issued only by senior management and requires lengthy review and sign-off. Going to the board or executive committee for every functional shift in an IP program may become tiresome; they may not understand what you're doing either.

Even if your policy process doesn't require high-level approval (an interesting issue in itself), you still ought to insist that a policy be a relatively short, high-level statement, providing clear, straightforward, enterprise-wide guidance, especially if it is going public or external. Structurally, the policy should *enable* and should generally refer to the subject matter of standards, procedures, and guidelines without actually cataloging them. The standards, procedures, and guidelines should cite the enabling authority.

Format and Content of an IP Policy

The actual format will probably be governed by whatever policy manual structures, if any, your enterprise uses. Above all else, make it readable. The tone should be personal and believable, especially for this type of policy. You're telling people that you expect them to behave in a way that may be uncomfortable. Show that you understand that; don't just command. Explain concisely why these measures are necessary and show that you realize an effort on their part is required.

As to content, the following list applies not just to policies but to standards, procedures, and guidelines as well. A given topic will probably be covered in a sentence or two in a policy. It may be the subject of an entire standard, and there could be several procedures and guidelines to support the standard.

Here's what to include in your IP policy:

- Introduction
  - —Purpose: What is this for?
  - —Definitions: See the Glossary of this book for likely candidates.
  - —Authority: Who's the prime mover behind this?
  - —Supporting background and rationale: Why do we need this? How did we get here and where are we going?
- Scope

—Types of information covered
—Types of information resources covered
—Organizational entities covered, including outside entities such as contractors, vendors, customers, and processing partners
—Types of threats addressed
—Exclusions (optional)
• Supporting specialist organizations
—Data security
—Continuity
—Combined functions and other support at the corporate (headquarters) level and lower levels
• General responsibilities
—Managers
—Owners
—Users
—Service suppliers
• Classification and declassification
—Continuity
—Security
• Risk assessment (optional)
—Type: qualitative, quantitative, monetarized
—Method: computer-based, manual, other
• Risk management (mandatory)
—Identification
—Acceptance
—Transferral (e.g., insurance or outside service)
—Mitigation
• Security and continuity strategies (preventive/reactive)
—Administrative
—Physical
—Logical
• Media control, declassification, and destruction (mention the need)
• Review and test
—Internal audit
—Security and continuity administration
—Quality assurance
—Peer review
—External review
• Enforcement and violation handling

- Education and training
- IP considerations in hiring, transfer, and separation
- Home and off-site use
- Policy (standard, etc.) revision and update process

There may be more subjects you wish to include. Certain of the topics mentioned above may appear elsewhere such as in human resources, financial, or technology policies or procedures. Some of the topics may not seem relevant, but before you drop them, think your decision through carefully.

I have created policies for clients that address the entire list in as few as five or six pages. Nor does every policy item require a separate supporting standard, procedure, or guideline. Many of those that do can be kept short.

IP Standards

I have a special skepticism about what ends up in a standards manual. Because I believe strongly in the standards process, I react strongly to its misuse.

A standard, in addition to describing a process or thing, is primarily used as a norm for measurement of compliance. For example, a standard tells you what it takes to send and receive television signals in a given country and what you must do to be in compliance with those requirements. Standards can be costly because they require:

- A measurement program
- An interpreter and arbitrator
- A submission for approval and deviation authorization process
- An authority and owner of the standard
- An enforcement process

If you don't have all that, you don't have a standards process, no matter what you call it.

Characteristics of Standards

Standards should have the following attributes:

- They should cover a critical subject of sufficient importance to warrant the effort. (I once read an article on whether plastic versus sewn noses should be a criterion for determining whether a stuffed, ursine animal was a true Teddy Bear. It may be very important to the bears and their collectors, but I wouldn't present it to the American National Standards Institute (ANSI) for formalization.)

• There should be a high cost associated with the consequences of nonstandardization.

• They should have a wide effect on the relevant population. (If only three people are affected, let them fight it out in the parking lot.)

• There should be multiple, viable, possible options. (There isn't much point in writing a standard for laws of gravity, since there's only one.)

• They should cover a long time span. (Don't write a standard for a process that is going to be obsolete or abandoned tomorrow.)

• They should be broadly applicable, otherwise, you end up with a very large number of individual standards.

• They should be enforceable.

• They shouldn't be overdone. In my opinion, about half of the corporate or institutional standards floating around are really procedures or guidelines dressed up in formal clothes or have no right to exist at all.

IP Procedures and Guidelines

Both procedures and guidelines deal with "how to," including how to comply with a standard. The standard states the requirements; the procedure or guideline indicates the process to be used. I believe the major distinction between the two is that procedures are usually mandatory and guidelines are advisory.

Deviations from standards should be possible, but they should be rather difficult to get approval for. Even though procedures are considered mandatory, it should be easier to get deviation approval for them and at a lower level of management. Guidelines, being advisory, should be the most flexible in this regard.

Both procedures and guidelines may be developed locally and modified to fit the circumstances. Standards are usually the result of a more global effort. Procedures and guidelines may (but not necessarily) apply for a shorter duration than a standard.

Like standards, procedures and guidelines require an interpreter and authority. To the extent they are mandatory, review and enforcement are necessary, but at a much lower level than for standards.

Procedures and guidelines, because of their specific and detailed how-to nature, may go on for page after page. There is a continuing argument about the level of detail to which a procedure or guideline should be written. One school, which I call the lowest possible denominator school, assumes no knowledge, no intelligence, and no motivation. The end product of this school is usually very long and pretty grim. The opposite end of the spectrum assumes knowledge and experience at least as great as, if not greater than, that of the author. This is the group that turns out procedures that read "Process accounts receivable"—period.

No single level of detail works everywhere. The most important determining factor regarding depth of detail and length is the nature of the audience for whom the procedure is being written—that is, their experience and familiarity with the process being described.

Some Guidelines for You

Auditors use standards, procedures, and even guidelines as measurements of control effectiveness. Read your procedures and ask how an auditor would read and interpret them. There's no point in making things so vague that the auditors won't be able to find specific violations. They'll just cite you for having vague standards and procedures.

Purity of process in the development of policies, standards, procedures, and guidelines has to be tempered by practical considerations, especially cost and resources. The doctrinally correct way, whatever that is, may not be the most practical way. On the other hand, the most practical way may not be the way that costs you the least. Find the way that accomplishes the objectives set out in the most cost-effective manner. Some compromise is implicit in that process.

Don't ever release a standard, procedure, or guideline without testing it out first on a sample of those who have to live with it. Role play and play "what-if." Try to teach someone new how to carry out the process described by following the procedures strictly as written. See what happens. Determine in advance how you're going to enforce the procedure. If everybody ignores it, what will you do? Will you even know?

Policies, standards, procedures, and guidelines do not promote or enforce themselves. They rely on management to do that. Unless you have responsible and affected management on your side before you take standards and procedures out for implementation, you may be digging yourself a large and uncomfortable hole. Psychology is generally on the side of the rebels. I have observed that when the battle lines are drawn between the bureaucrats (not necessarily staff bureaucrats) who developed the procedure or standard and the "loose cannons" who do not want to adopt them, the loose cannons often win. The mere fact that such epithets are in play indicates that the air needs to be cleared.

Mission Statements and Job Descriptions

There are two instances when IP-related mission statements and job descriptions are appropriate:

1. For IP specialist departments and individuals.
2. To include IP content in nonspecialized missions and job descriptions. In this case, the users, owners, and service suppliers would be covered as well as IP-related staffs such as human relations, general security, legal, external relations, MIS, and telecommunications.

Mission statements serve three general purposes:

1. Organizational planning
2. Individual and group guidance and performance
3. Measurement

They should be designed to serve all three goals.

Assuming that your organization places any credence at all in the use and value of mission statements and job descriptions, there are several characteristics you should seek to develop:

• *A sense of priorities.* Mission statements that are laundry lists of every possible responsibility are usually greeted with the disdain they deserve. If **security** is a part-time function, build your security requirements into the overall context of the job being performed by the present incumbents. If the job is full-time and brand new, it is even more important to establish a sense of proportion about what is really important and what is not.

• *Ongoing targets.* Write mission statements and job descriptions with the ongoing environment as a target. Start-up tasks and special projects should be reserved for individual agreements and setting periodic goals and objectives.

• *Measurability.* Write the statements and descriptions in terms that can be measured at least qualitatively, if not quantitatively, and as unambiguously as possible. This is for your benefit as well as the assignee's. People are much more secure and effective if they can determine for themselves whether they are doing a good job and can have a reasonable expectation that management, using the same yardstick, will arrive at the same conclusion. Even if there is a disagreement, you are both starting from the same basic set of requirements in beginning your discussions. After you've developed your job descriptions, ask the incumbents or potential incumbents to play back their understandings and compare them to your intentions. You may be surprised.

• *Feasibility.* Make sure that the functions, relationships, and work to be performed can be carried out by the people and organizational structures to which they've been assigned. Be especially cognizant of the skills, experience, job levels, and pay scales of the individuals and the classes of responsibilities they would normally be expected to take on. Don't try to assign tasks to a first-line manager that would normally belong to a vice-president.

Remember that the population of individuals you are working with is normally small and the number of tasks large. The temptation to get all the work assigned to someone can often produce some unrealistic mission statements and job descriptions. Don't try to solve a resource problem by writing unreasonable missions and descriptions.

• Cultural appropriateness. Make sure the jobs and missions fit the culture of your organization. By all means, seek guidance from other enterprises and sources, but test each element described against your own requirements and priorities before you accept them.

Some Examples

Here are some sample specialist and nonspecialist department mission statements and individual job descriptions. They're composites and interpretations, not direct citations.

Each description states a set of functional duties. Obviously, the scope of the department's or individual's activities will be, in part, a function of the organizational level at which they operate. Whether one or more people perform these functions full-time or part-time depends on scope, organization, and workload. The order of the items does not necessarily imply priority, but you can assume that items included in the list are common to most enterprises with a viable IP program.

Data Security Administration (Staff—Corporate, Division, or Department)

- Develop and maintain information security policy, standards, guidelines, and procedures.
- Develop awareness and training programs, including materials.
- Develop information security strategies, plans, staffing requirements, budgets, and priorities.
- May conduct information security tests, penetration studies, and assessments. (Internal **EDP audit** is an alternative source.)
- May administer violation process. (Adjudication and disposition of actual violations are line-management responsibilities.)
- May administer access control authorization process. (This may be a separate group or may be handled by each user department or by MIS.)
- May supervise specification and selection of security technology, e.g., access control facilities and encryption. (If not supervision, then at least some level of sign-off.)
- Review security characteristics of proposed **system,** telecommunications, and application hardware and software.
- Develop risk scenarios and vulnerability studies.
- Advise on and, as necessary, participate in responding to attacks, viruses, and other security exposures.
- Advise management (including the audit committee) on the state of enterprise information security.
- May represent the enterprise professionally, as necessary, to outside organizations, regulators, the press, and the public on matters dealing with information security.

Continuity Administration (Staff—Corporate, Division, or Department)

- Develop and maintain **continuity** policy, standards, guidelines, and procedures.

- Develop overall information continuity strategies, plans, staffing requirements, budgets, and priorities.
- Supervise or direct the development of specific contingency and disaster prevention plans. (Depending on the enterprise's priorities, these may be related to data centers or information systems or, ideally, they may cover business resumption in its fullest scope.)
- Test and evaluate these plans.
- Develop awareness and training programs, including materials.
- Develop and supervise processing and data backup storage programs, including site selection, media management, and staffing.
- May negotiate contracts with third parties to provide backup facilities, as necessary.
- May supervise specification and selection of preventive and backup continuity technology, e.g., alarms, sensors, fire extinguishers, backup power. (If not supervision, then at least some level of sign-off.)
- Review continuity characteristics of proposed system, telecommunications, and **application** hardware and software.
- Develop risk scenarios and vulnerability studies.
- Advise on and, as necessary, participate in responding to actual outages and other continuity exposures.
- Advise management (including the audit committee) on the state of enterprise information continuity.
- May represent the enterprise professionally, as necessary, to outside organizations, regulators, the press, and the public on matters dealing with information continuity.

Information Protection Administration (Staff—Corporate, Division, or Department)

- A composite of the two missions outlined above.

Obviously, you can break these functions down into multiple subgroups. There are other functions, such as insurance, personal security, and fraud detection that also relate to the functions mentioned above.

Organizational Interrelationships

Perhaps the most frequently debated relationship is that of internal audit to security and continuity (IP). This relationship is often conditioned by the skills, leverage, priorities, and workload of internal audit. In addition, some enterprises limit the role of internal audit to financially material systems; others do not.

I have seen many variations on the theme, but the important point to remember is that internal audit's mission is assessment, not implementation. You cannot expect internal audit to design, plan, or run your IP program. It may have strong opinions on what you need to do and you may, therefore, think that it is designing the program by default. However, no internal auditors I have ever known would take direct responsibility for IP program management, nor should they.

Other functional groups within the enterprise that have a bearing on IP include:

- *MIS.* Especially change management, systems and applications design, quality assurance, operations, technical support, library management, and database management.
- *Telecommunications.* Including voice and data.
- *Data administration.* Has a strategic and tactical planning, as well as a standards-setting, role to perform and is a key element in both security and continuity.
- *Other.* These include legal, human resources, general security, public and labor relations, finance and administration, and facilities management.

How Much Is Enough?

For a fully effective program, all of the functions discussed in this chapter should be present, but the degree to which you carry them out is strongly conditioned by your business needs. A large information-dependent enterprise with widely distributed information processing facilities, armies of users, scores of developers, and mission-critical applications is obviously in a totally different dimension from a small or intermediate business that wants to protect a couple of personal computers (PCs). In the former case, take the mission statements and job descriptions quite literally. In the latter, examine the protective results you want to achieve and determine how you want to go about it. Often, you may find that you need little more than a change of perspective on the part of the PC users.

In any event, size is not a reliable measure of bureaucracy. I know some one-person bureaucrats, even though that term sounds contradictory. What makes the difference is efficiency and effectiveness. You can achieve (or miss) that goal at practically any size. Just make sure that whatever you do is appropriate to your needs.

13

Using Architectures to Develop Well-Protected Information Systems

---

What's in this chapter?

- Information Protection Architectures
  —When Do You Need an IP Architecture?
  —Characteristics of an IP Architecture
- The Development Process

In the early 1980s, an occasional information **security** or contingency planning specialist might have been seen shedding a tear because there were no security or contingency worlds left to conquer. Perhaps more accurately, their discontent sprang from a realization that the status quo of **information protection** (IP) seemed destined to remain exactly that. There was more security technology on the market than the market wanted. There were four major, and a larger number of minor, access control facilities sharing the mainframe installed base. The typical data center was a small fortress. There were backup sites aplenty if you had the right brands of hardware and systems software.

This is not to say that the information processing world was all that well protected. Installed but unused access control facilities were the order of the day (and can still be found). Written but untested contingency plans abounded (and still do). Unfortunately, the moti-

Note: This chapter is adapted and expanded from an article I wrote for *Information Security Product News* (September 1990).

vation to improve or expand on these conditions in most organizations was slight to nonexistent.

But times are changing. More and more senior operating and information processing executives are becoming acutely aware of a protection dilemma. On the one hand, their enterprises have become deeply dependent on information processing systems, to the point where **system** downtime can impact the bottom line. On the other hand, management information systems (MIS) management's central control over the enterprise's information processing resources has been diluted by distributed processing, autonomous systems on varied technological **platforms,** networks, outsourcing, powerful workstations, and the like. Just when the enterprise needs a basis for consistent control most, it seems to have it least.

In most organizations, in spite of occasional moves to reconsolidate, the all-powerful MIS organization that owned, directed, and ran everything seems to have gone the way of the Berlin Wall. But the pendulum does seem to be making a swing back to centralized direction in a different and interesting way.

For designing systems and **applications** protection in this new, freer environment, an increasing number of organizations are pursuing security and **continuity** architectures and designs that are stated in terms of objectives and requirements rather than direct technological and administrative procedures that must be rigidly implemented. The senior management of these organizations seems to be saying, "We need consistent, complete, cost-effective, adaptable, responsive information protection. The appropriate level and state of protection is paramount. You can choose how you get there, but the end result must meet specifications."

To achieve this flexibility, the specifications themselves must accommodate a variety of current and planned processing environments. This actually bodes well for improved security and continuity. In the past, comparatively rigid security and continuity criteria would sustain most of the damage in any head-on collisions with other design criteria such as ease of use, transaction throughput, database flexibility, and ease of access. The reasons for this would vary—technological, economic, operational, or political. But they added up to a perception that information protection was a drag on productivity. That perception needs to be overcome if an IP program is going to succeed. Flexible protection architectures can help.

Information Protection Architectures

An information protection architecture is a statement of overall design and operating objectives for the security, continuity, and **control** of the **information resources** it encompasses.

The primary purpose of *any* architectural statement is to ensure a common level of understanding and a common basis for design and implementation by all groups sharing the same information resources. The more widespread and complex the sharing becomes, the more important it is to have architectures. You can expect to have a variety of architectures and subarchitectures concerned with the design of documents, screens and menus, data and databases, networks, applications, and systems.

Architectural influence surfaces in different contexts. The most common are languages; document and data structures; and process, data exchange, and control interfaces. To be effective, any architecture must reflect the policies, business functions, and technology of the enterprise. (See Figure 13-1.)

Suppose you don't have architectures? Actually, you probably do. You may not have a formal structure, but if you're processing data through interrelated applications, shared or common databases, connected systems, and telecommunications, you have some default architectures in place. In most cases, they're probably vendor supplied and determined. The overall result may not be as elegant, cost-effective, consistent, or adaptable as you desire, but architectures do exist, and they need to be surfaced, described, understood, and validated before beginning new development.

To encompass the full scope of information protection as we've defined it really requires three highly related subarchitectures:

1. Areas dealing with integrity and confidentiality are usually included under a security architecture. Access control is the mainstay process.

2. To deal with disruption, I'd like to use the term *continuity*, which includes both preventive and reactive components. A continuity architecture, plan, and design provide a more comprehensive approach to disruption than contingency or disaster recovery planning alone. In the 1990s, because there are so many critical systems and networks with short "mean time to pain" indexes, failure reduction is getting a higher priority than backup.

Figure 13-1. The architecture-based security implementation process.

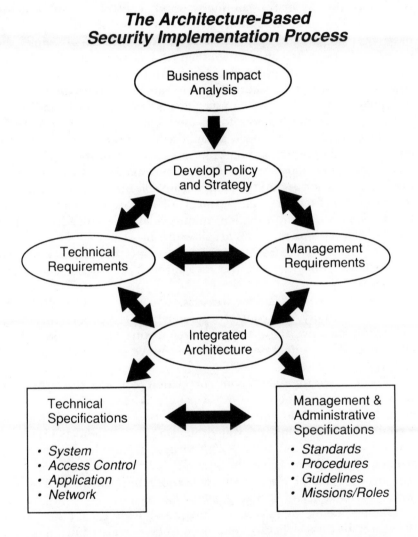

The Architecture-Based
Security Implementation Process

3. A related and highly important architectural area is business and accounting controls. For the same reasons that motivate its security and continuity concerns, management is also showing increasing interest in maintaining consistent, complete, and effective controls on the quality of **information** and correctness of processing.

An architecture presupposes the existence of some overall policy and strategy base. The policy generally outlines management's desires regarding the security, continuity, and control of information resources. The strategy outlines at an enterprise or extended enterprise level the general approaches to be followed. For example, the policy may state that once established, the same security level must be maintained by all users of a specific information resource. The strategy may state that security criteria will be centrally determined, the application of the criteria to specific resources will be by individual owners, and the mechanisms to be used will be jointly determined.

Once you have developed a commonly accepted and understood enterprise-wide protection policy, it becomes part of the platform for architectural development. Your other information systems architectures form a major part of the platform as well. Information protection is a derivative function, gaining much of its specific character from the ways in which information resources are developed and used overall. Never develop an IP architecture in isolation.

As your architecture begins to take shape, the strategy of how to get there from here will also take form. The process is iterative, not linear.

For resource and timing reasons, you may wish to deal with security, continuity, and control separately. However, once they exist, to be truly effective these three subarchitectures need to be at least correlated, if not integrated, before you move on to actual development.

To illustrate the point about correlation, consider the virus. The virus is a security issue. How did it get in? Where is it? How do you get rid of it? How do you keep other viruses out? The virus is also a continuity issue. How do you protect against its effects? How do you recover from its impact? The virus can also have accounting control implications. Have the accuracy and completeness of your data been impaired? Have your applications been affected? You can create a similar set of scenarios about hackers.

Besides being correlated or integrated with each other, these three architectural structures also need to be correlated or integrated with the overall document, data, system, application, and network architectures of the enterprise or extended enterprise. This is fine if you're developing major new systems and applications. But suppose you want to upgrade, retrofit, or reengineer the security, continuity, or accounting controls in existing systems? Even here, a somewhat shorter excursion into architectural statements can assist in clarifying the process you're working with and the targets you're trying to hit.

When Do You Need an IP Architecture?

Some of the key indicators that would suggest you need a protection architecture are:

• *Multilevel technology.* This includes mainframes acting as processors and file servers; minis performing the same functions plus network control and management; and micros as workstations, controllers, and file servers.

• *Telecommunications* in single or multienterprise networks using local and/or wide area facilities.

• *Multiple business functions* operating in an integrated fashion.

• *Data sharing* by multiple organizations, users, systems, and applications.

• *External users and processing partners*—the so-called extended enterprise. This includes but is not limited to electronic funds transfer, electronic data interchange, point of sale, and reservations systems. Even electronic mail can reach the levels of functional richness and variety that require protection and control architectures.

• *Rapid development and modification of applications and systems.* For example, service organizations such as banks and transportation companies offer a constantly changing and bewildering array of services, terms, and conditions to their customers. To carry this off, new applications, system configurations, and networks often must be designed, developed, tested, and deployed in record time. Protection and controls often slip. Architecture-based design standards can make the inclusion of protective and control factors easier. Any organization that uses its information systems to bring new, competitive offerings into the market rapidly may be in this category.

• A *lowest-common-denominator approach* to controlling access to all of your systems and applications. If you're allowing the system and application with the least demand for controls to govern the control structure, you may need a protection architecture.

Characteristics of an IP Architecture

An IP architecture must have consistent and coherent design criteria for including security mechanisms at appropriate points on the access paths between users and resources. It must provide a sufficient range of design criteria to ensure that appropriate integrity, quality, accountability, and audit functions are being performed. It must also address appropriate preventive and reactive continuity mechanisms to deal with loss of service in all processing and transmission points supporting critical business functions. It must provide common functional appearances to all users, such as log-on procedures, warnings, labels, and menus.

In a large multisystem environment, unless you employ some form of scope reduction and prioritizing, architectural development can become lengthy and unwieldy. The objective of the exercise is well-protected systems, not architecture for its own sake. Large multisystem environments need not involve large systems. If you hook up enough local area networks (LANs), minis, and micros you can create a very interesting architectural scenario. To see practical results early, however, you may have to limit the scope. Comprehensive does not mean universal. Cost-effective *does* mean that the important systems and applications come first.

Although you will see many common characteristics from enterprise to enterprise, unfortunately there is no universally applicable IP architecture.

An IP architecture must correlate and integrate with your other current or planned information systems architectures. It begins life as a set of design objectives stated in terms of what and whom you wish to control, why, and to what degree. But architecture won't do it alone. To turn it into a functioning reality, you need two major underpinnings:

1. *Enterprise-wide policies and standards* for security, continuity, and control in application and system design. In the case of security, for example, this includes the administrative as well as technology-based security measures.

2. *Development methodologies* that will assist in the integration of security, continuity, and control into the system and application along with function, performance, capacity, user-friendliness, and other required characteristics. There are several to consider:

- Systems development life cycle methodologies, which provide an orderly and comprehensive path of progression from business goals and objectives to fully operational information processing systems.

- Computer-assisted software engineering (CASE), which is a structured system for programming development that provides tools to produce consistent and modular software based on data structure, usage, and process flow analysis. It can make programmers more productive, make maintenance easier, provide consistent documentation, and often develop higher quality running code faster than more conventional development methods. The downside is the cost of learning and moving to the technique and some of the apparent rigidities in usage. CASE requires a significant investment and is best adopted incrementally. It can, however, provide significant benefits, especially in new development. Using it for maintaining existing systems may require more adjustment and retrofit than it's worth.
- Packaged software. Here the security, continuity, and control *development* criteria and requirements must be converted to *selection and adaptation* criteria.

These can greatly enhance your development efforts, but before signing up for any specific products or methodologies (and there are many), ask for demonstrable proof that security, continuity, and control are major design features in the methodologies and packages themselves and in the systems and applications they produce.

Unfortunately, the companies producing these offerings are market driven and, until recently, the market hasn't been clamoring for protective measures. Ask for examples and references. Get them to explain how security, for example, will be supported.

The Development Process

The following steps outline the architectural approach to security, continuity, and controls development:

1. Understand the existing environment for the enterprise (or extended enterprise, if you're dealing with functions such as electronic funds transfer or electronic data interchange):

- Business objectives, critical success factors, essential business functions, information requirements.

- Technical environment, including the system architecture, hardware, software, major applications, networks, and technology plans.
- Organizational, budget, legal, and regulatory considerations.
- Current levels of information protection.
- Other areas that may have an effect.

2. For the enterprise or enterprise group, perform a business impact analysis for security and continuity. Create control objectives for critical business functions, data, systems, and applications. Identify and prioritize the business functions and applications that are critical to security, continuity, or control. They won't always be the same. Be careful. Not every application within a critical business function is itself critical. There may also be critical supporting applications in noncritical business functions. What hardware, software, telecommunications, and administrative activities support those applications?

3. Develop architectural objectives based on the varying degrees of security, continuity, and control required by these critical functions and applications. Define a baseline level of security, continuity, and control for noncritical environments. Answer two fundamental questions:

- What will security, continuity, and control achieve?
- How will it be achieved?

4. Develop security, continuity, and control requirements in management and technical terms:

- *Management.* Standards and procedures for users, developers, and administrators. For example: On what basis will you deploy security and continuity administration—central? distributed? business function? enterprise-wide? organizational levels? hybrid?
- *Technical.* For example: Security consideration would include access control software and hardware and other system software including database and network and application-specific software and hardware. Include development, library management, performance, change management, and deployment tools.

5. Develop security, continuity, and control specifications. Security specifications would cover authorization, identification, verification, access control, accountability, and auditability.

6. State these architecture-based requirements and specifications in a documented form that can be utilized by development teams and incorporated into CASE tool functions.

7. Develop walk-through and test criteria for measurement of compliance with the architecture, standards, specifications, and requirements.

8. Develop maintenance and update procedures (change management) that ensure that the integrity of the control and security process is being maintained along with the continuity characteristics. Software is dynamic stuff, and poorly controlled change management can alter the entire character of an application or system.

Maintenance doesn't just mean fixes; it means change—new transactions, new users, new platforms, new hardware. They all make their way into the baseline systems and applications and require change. *Stable software is a good sign of a dormant enterprise.*

In dealing with maintenance, you are looking for assurances that only management-authorized changes are being made by management-authorized people. You also must determine that those changes, in addition to being effective, efficient, and functionally appropriate, either maintain or enhance the security, control, and continuity characteristics of the system or application. Doing this usually involves walk-through reviews, tests, and sign-offs prior to deploying the change.

I believe that maintenance is one of the most important, dangerous, and underrated areas of the development process. It is often regarded as the KP duty of systems or applications development and foisted off on junior members of the team while the more experienced members "create and design." Lousy maintenance has caused more security and control problems than hackers.

This architecture-based design and development process may extend beyond the bounds of a single enterprise. In fact, architecture becomes almost mandatory in the extended enterprise environment, even if a single organization is providing all the design and development. Unique deployment, operational, management, administrative, and audit issues will still arise in each member enterprise even though you're all using the same designs.

Is architectural development a major undertaking? Yes, but it can have a major positive effect on the protection of the enterprise's information resources. The time and resources required will vary with the scope of business functions, systems, and applications to be covered.

To be effective it must involve more than security, continuity, and control specialists. It must involve the key individuals concerned in the design, development, deployment, and operation of critical applications and systems.

If properly scoped, well-planned, and appropriately designed, an information protection architecture, once established, need not be implemented in one shot. To minimize impact and ensure effectiveness, it probably should be brought on stream in phases. It's not a trivial investment. However, it can be a very cost-effective step in developing the basis for stable, secure, well-controlled processing platforms for future business growth.

People and Protection—Making the Unnatural Natural

14

Information Ethics

Ethical behavior toward **information** and **information resources** doesn't come naturally to most people. An effective ethics program must take people as they are and provide guidance on how you want them to behave. The more "unnatural" that behavior seems to the individual, the more extensive and pragmatic the program must be. In this chapter, I illustrate why this lack of naturalness exists, what the implications are for information ethics, and how, on a practical basis, an information ethics program can cope with the situation.

By claiming that ethical behavior toward information is unnatural, I'm not suggesting that human beings are not fundamentally ethical. I believe that, on the whole, we are. I do mean that *the rules of ethical behavior are not intuitively obvious when it comes to information.* That represents a problem to managers, users, and protectors of information resources. As a manager, you'll have to state your ethical expectations more explicitly and enforce them more actively than you do for protecting tangible assets.

In many cases, the first problem is getting people to look at information as an asset at all. To most individuals, information is in an amorphous class of its own. We've all heard, for instance, that "knowledge means power." However, we seldom take that statement to its logical conclusion and establish a direct asset value for that knowledge. In the first place, it's not easy to do. Second, somehow it doesn't feel natural. It's a mistake to assume that people will automatically apply their norms of ethical behavior about tangible assets to information.

What are your ethical expectations when it comes to information? How do you expect your employees to behave? Consciously or unconsciously, we all make mental judgments about the characters of the people we work with, usually using our own attitudes (and possibly our behavior) as the standard.

Where you set your expectations will obviously affect the entire nature of your **information protection** (IP) program. Either extreme can be dangerous. When it comes to information protection, believing that everyone has the highest ethical concern and the practical knowledge to back it up is naive. The converse, however, can reduce your department, division, or enterprise to the equivalent of an armed camp. Trust is an important component in any IP program because, as I've stressed over and over, you can't and shouldn't try to protect everything against everyone.

Ethics and Technology

You need to develop and publicly state what your expectations are. It's unlikely that a few generic statements about behavior toward information will be enough, leaving it to the individual to fill in the blanks. Technology has made it difficult for most individuals to develop, on their own, an appropriate and sharply focused information ethics code. Why? The following four reasons are the most basic.

1. Ethics focuses on our relations with others and their property. Information technology can alter existing relationships and create new and unfamiliar relationships.
2. Intangible property is different, and electronics has made that difference even more difficult to deal with.
3. There is a collision of rights concerning information. Freedom of expression, freedom of information, privacy, and protection of intellectual property often conflict. Sorting out priorities is difficult, especially in electronic environments.
4. There is a conflict between our natural urge to communicate and our urge to protect property.

Information Technology and Relationships

Depersonalization is probably the most obvious way electronics can influence relationships. Every day, more electronic systems or processes are replacing person-to-person transactions. That's what we had in mind when we started using computers and networks, but the sense of obligation that we would feel toward a human partner is reduced in the process. This is especially true when you need human intervention and can't get it. If you can't identify another person in the transaction, your sense of personal responsibility may shrink and your sense of indignation and frustration may rise.

Anonymity is another example. Haven't you at one time or another in your life wanted to be invisible? One of the electronically produced conditions that permit hackers to behave as they do is the ability to hide behind some false identity. There's an even more interesting corollary in the case of viruses. Although hackers know who their victims are and may be known by their victims, virus attackers operate differently. With viruses, not only are the attackers unknown to the victims, but the victims are usually unidentified to the culprits as well. The situation is double blind. Virus attackers can ease their consciences by claiming that they didn't know the specific outcomes or victims. So even though they have been irresponsible, they can rationalize that they certainly didn't intend to cause someone to lose millions or miss an important event or lose his or her life.

In summary, electronics can weaken positive relationships and strengthen negative ones. You must deal with that if your ethics program is going to be effective.

The Intangible Property Difference

Establishing ownership of intangible property is difficult, and sometimes it has to be arbitrary. Finding the "true" owner can be more trouble than its worth. Consider a database consolidated from several sources and used by a variety of departments: Try to determine who the owner is, who the authors are, and who has rights to look, change, copy, or destroy. When you distribute that same data over a large number of processors where other individuals can make alterations, additions, and deletions, what's happening to the property rights of the authors and owners?

Unfortunately, a primary component of any property-related ethics program is knowing who the owners are and what their rights are, which is not easy with electronics.

For another good example of the dilemma, read some of the discussions on audio and videotape copying or software piracy. You can make a legitimate case for a very wide range of actions.

Collision of Rights

Some of our guiding principles, such as freedom of information and rights of privacy, conflict in specific situations. Which is more important, your right to privacy or the public's right to know? The answer usually depends on whether you're the affected party or the knowledge seeker. That's human nature! Don't force people into double-bind ethical situations by making it impossible for them to satisfy their own consciences about the behavior you expect.

The law is not very clear in these areas. The legal concept of intellectual property has gotten most of its exercise through copyright and trade secret disputes. It's stretching things to try to cover the vast amounts of information that you may want to keep proprietary with copyright or trade secret provisions. If the law isn't clear and people's intuition isn't clear, then some external guidance is called for—from you!

Communicate or Keep Secret?

Our natural urge is to protect private property but to share information. To illustrate my point, let me introduce you to my granddaughter, Sarah Lynn, and her puppy, Gizmo. At the time of this writing, Sarah is a little more than two years old and Gizmo is about six months old. When it comes to things, they both have a very strong sense of ownership. Sarah is quite eloquent in telling you that things are *"mine."* Don't try to take a bone or rubber toy from Gizmo. But both Sarah and Gizmo have also learned to communicate very well and do so incessantly. They are two of the most inquisitive creatures I have ever met. Their noses are into everything. The natural urge of human beings (and puppies) is to communicate and find out. Keeping secrets is unnatural.

We also regard information as part of a general transactional relationship. You trust me; I trust you. You tell me important things; I reciprocate. That relationship is not always based on a need to know; it's more frequently based on a "want to know" and mutual accommodation. It also involves personal trust. As a matter of fact, most of us feel a bit offended about the need-to-know process. Curiosity (intellectual or otherwise) is a very powerful drive. Since electronics makes it so much easier to pass information on, this mutual accommodation is made that much easier, and the need-to-know criterion seems that much more restrictive. Further, we all have a natural suspicion of individuals or organizations that are secretive.

The Information Ethics Program

Consider the following guidelines when developing your information ethics program:

1. *Make the scope realistic.* Any successful information ethics program must take the human realities into account. You can't expect people to be perfect models of restraint under any circumstance or to meet your expectations without guidance, direction, and management. This takes time, effort, and expense. So set realistic goals and objectives and direct the program to those areas that really count. Overly ambitious ethics programs and **security** programs usually collapse under their own weight.

2. *Make it specific to your organization.* Unless the individuals whose behavior you want to influence see themselves and their environment clearly in the directions you're giving, they won't respond. Philosophical statements are fine for preambles, but the more localized, specific, and applicable the rules are, the more likely they are to be carried out.

3. *Role play.* After you've defined information ethics objectives and designed a program, try the concepts and approach out on some of the managers and employees who will have to live with it, before implementing it. Here's where the conflicts, ambiguities, and hostilities will rise to the surface. You'll get reactions you never dreamed of—positive and negative.

4. *Determine what you are really saying.* Search out the implications of what you are proposing. This is related to role playing, but you can do this on your own, if you like. Consultants can often be helpful in this area. As examples, consider these two terms:

- *Need to know.* How will you determine it? How will you arbitrate? How will you enforce it? If the answers aren't clear and practical, don't use it as a principle.
- *Information owner.* How is this determined? How arbitrated? How enforced? Again, if it can't be supported, find a different platform.

Some organizations can or are required to adopt these and other principles; others have great difficulty. Don't pick up someone else's ethics and security program indiscriminately. Make sure it fits, or it won't work. Worse yet, it may work at a cost you don't want to pay.

5. *Make the ethical codes guide, not trap.* You are trying to direct and guide behavior, not create snares to catch people. Enforce with punitive measures as necessary, but a high body count is not the sign of a successful ethics program. As a matter of fact, if you continue to have a large number of offenders, your ethics program is a failure. You also have no right to demand behavior that society would generally regard as unreasonable unless a correspondingly strong rationale (national defense, protection of life) exists.

6. *Involve local management directly and extensively.* Senior management's support is important as a background. Local management will make it work. This is especially important with awareness programs. Unless an individual believes that his or her direct management and peers are buying in, he or she won't respond. A road show made up of strangers from headquarters won't work; a local program with joint participation by the experts and local management will.

7. *Use peer pressure.* The objective is to make personal commitment and peer pressure the most powerful motivators. The "buy-in" is transmitted by actions and examples, not directives and formal communications. Use the natural leaders within your departments and divisions. Create an atmosphere where peer pressure supports personal commitment.

8. *Get commitment by example.* Actions do speak louder than words. The organization, its management, and its employees all demonstrate their commitment to information ethics not by the number of posters, the size of the policy section, or the frequency of classes, but by their daily activities. That's how you should measure success, and that's how you should demonstrate to your processing partners and the rest of the outside world that information ethics, natural or not, is part of your operating procedure.

15

Awareness and Training

What's in this chapter?

- Characteristics of a Successful Program
- Variations on Awareness Programs
- Getting Senior Management's Attention and Support
- Getting Other Management's Attention and Support
- Presenting Information Protection Positively

You need an **information protection** (IP) awareness program because you are asking people to do things that, by and large, lie outside their normal modes of behavior. So you must motivate them by showing them compelling reasons for IP, and you must educate them about what you want done. The more out of the ordinary or abnormal they consider the behavior you want, the more effort and energy you'll have to expend to achieve it. In short, don't expect information protection unless you make clear what you want and how much you want it.

What's the difference between an awareness program and a training program? At first glance, the answer might seem to be that awareness is for motivation and training is for education. That's right, up to a point. But an awareness program, designed primarily to motivate, should certainly tell people *what* you want them to do as well as *why*. A training program teaches the more in-depth procedural and design activities. However, you should never teach the *what* without the *why*. It's a matter of proportion.

Put another way, awareness is for everybody. Training is for those with a specific need. So the baseline procedural knowledge you want everyone to have should be incorporated into the awareness program.

Will a single type of program suffice? In many organizations, yes. In large or dispersed enterprises with diverse information-related functions, probably not. Will any program, offered only once, suffice? I seriously doubt it. Personnel turnover makes success through a one-shot effort unlikely, and you also have the reinforcement issue to deal with.

Characteristics of a Successful Program

In the following pages, I outline some variations on awareness and training themes. They are intended to be illustrative; only a few organizations need or should do them all. Pick the ones you require and tailor them to your needs. But first, there are some questions you should answer:

• What are the major IP objectives you want to attain? Try to make these as specific as possible to the current situation of the organization.

• What groups and individuals are critical to the attainment?

• What are their current attitudes and levels of knowledge about IP?

• Do they share enough common experience, background, interest, motivation, and organizational responsibilities to make a common awareness program effective?

• Are there certain mission-critical groups that require special instruction? You can consider this by occupational specialty (e.g., programmers, systems and applications designers, management information systems (MIS) operations, security specialists) or level of responsibility (e.g., senior management, line management, entry-level personnel).

• What forms do you want the program to take? Besides classes, are there other established vehicles you can use, such as company newsletters, contests, staff sessions, retreats, video reports, bulletin boards, or giveaways to help get your message across?

Don't get carried away by the communications process. I've known managers and security specialists to become so entranced with the idea of making a movie or video that they lose all sense of why they are doing it or what else they need to get done.

Catchy slogans are great but you can only communicate so much with a slogan. Slogans also have a relatively short shelf life.

• Who can you count on to help develop, present, and manage the program? Don't expect management to create a program itself, but do make it possible for management to participate in a way that supports the program and its credibility. Choose management representatives who are articulate, positive, knowledgeable, and, most important, respected. Use top management to the extent it's appropriate in your enterprise.

• What are you trying to get across? Fundamentally, the basic elements of your IP program. You are trying to influence behavior, so tailor your presentations toward the rationale for IP *in your enterprise.* Generalized threats have impact only if the individuals can see the application to themselves.

Don't just lay out principles. Give tangible action steps. "The Importance of Data Classification" is a topic for an IP professional seminar. "The Three Basic Categories of Data Classification in US-GUYS Inc. and How to Use Them" is a topic for an awareness program. "Viruses, a New and Deadly Information Threat," in addition to being overly dramatic is far less effective than, "The US-GUYS Anti-Viral Program and Your Part in It."

Give them something to take with them. This should not be just a copy of the policy, standards, and guidelines. Some type of giveaway that will serve as a reminder of what the program is all about is a good idea.

Entertain, up to a limit. IP as a topic can use lightening up, but don't make it look silly or frivolous. It is a serious issue. Don't make fun of people, unless it's yourself. A few war stories are helpful, provided they are credible, have some pertinence to your topic, and don't make the individuals involved look stupid.

There are plenty of generalized tapes, films, posters, and documents available, and some are quite good. Use them as supplements.

Good as these support items may be, they are not your program. They are ingredients. You can buy many of the components for a successful program and get professional assistance. But when the dinner is served, make sure you were the chef. Awareness programs should never be totally catered affairs.

Variations on Awareness Programs

There are different types of awareness programs geared toward specific audiences:

• *Executive awareness.* You may want to develop an executive awareness program in order to get approval, funding, and resources for developing a program. In any event, it is key that top management understand, approve, and support your IP efforts. If you don't need it to get going, still make it part of your early efforts. You may want to provide a special program for the audit committee of the board of directors.

• *Middle-management awareness.* This is the level that is absolutely key to your success. They are your peers and immediate subordinates. There are two schools of thought on special sessions for middle managers. One says, "Keep them in with the troops to show solidarity. The leaders must be visible to those being led." The other says, "It's important to discuss the hows and whys, pluses and minuses, of a program like this, frankly and openly, with members of management. You can't do that in front of the troops." I agree with both camps. My advice, if you can pull it off, is to do both. The ideal situation is to hold a session for middle managers and then involve them directly in presenting part of the program to their people.

• *Technical specialists.* These are designers, programmers, operations specialists, local area network (LAN) managers, telecommunications specialists, and others. These folks have special missions and special contributions to make to IP. If you can, treat them separately. There are technical issues that they would probably like to discuss in detail that would befuddle or bore a general audience.

• *Security and continuity specialists (including internal audit).* Do they need a separate program? If there are enough of them and you want to clearly outline their roles in the overall program, yes. All of your specialists should be fully aware of the other programs you are offering, especially as those programs affect their jobs. Don't accidentally mouse-trap a specialist by publicly referring all future issues to him or her without giving the specialist a chance to explore the implications.

• *General user and owner populations.* This is your mainstream start-up program. Aim it at the "knowledge worker" who typifies the group. If there are wide variances in the level, background, experience, and criticality of the groups, you may have to subdivide the sessions and alter some of the content and technique. Above all, don't insult or overwhelm your audience.

• *The new employee program.* This is probably a slightly modified version of the previous program, taking into account the relative newness of the individuals to the company and the program. How frequently you run one of these depends on your rate of hire. There are several dangers here. You may be hiring new managers, new technicians, new users. Their **security** and **continuity** perspectives are different. Don't lump them together.

• *The refresher program.* Once is not enough, but more than once of the same thing can be deadly. Plan something new for each program. This is where a guest speaker or a contest or a new giveaway can be very helpful. People may have lousy memories for security procedures, but they'll remember every slide you showed in your first program if you show them again.

Not every enterprise needs all of these, and certainly each company needs to determine how often a program should be offered. I have made awareness programs synonymous with live sessions or classes. There are programs that are strictly publications based, and sometimes they're necessary because of costs, labor contracts, fragmented organization and locations, or other reasons. I believe that the personal touch in this area is extremely important. Discussion of the reasons and the methods behind an IP program can happen only in some kind of organized session. If it's impossible, so be it. But try to get a live training program approved.

Getting Senior Management's Attention and Support

Follow these steps to ensure top management's cooperation:

• Have a specific program in mind. Don't come in without a plan.
• Research other protection programs, but don't copy wholesale.
• Research other types of awareness programs (e.g., safety or drug programs run by your organization), especially the failures.
• Keep it manageable.
• Know what it will cost (including lost labor time).
• Justify it (not necessarily cost justify).
• Search out objections beforehand.
• If possible, get an operating executive as sponsor.
• Ask for public endorsement by top management to use in dealing with other managers in the organization.
• Find out what your competitors are (or aren't) doing.

Getting Other Management's Attention and Support

You can't succeed unless the other managers are on your side. They'll respond if you:

- Make sure you have their management's (senior management) active support.
- Don't farm it out to the staff specialists for total execution.
- Involve them in program development.
- Tailor the program to the local unit.
- Include the manager as an active participant.
- Test on volunteers before you launch. Don't treat units as guinea pigs. Their time is too valuable.
- When you assign local responsibility, show how you will assist. A program that says, "It's your responsibility" and stops there is in trouble.

Presenting Information Protection Positively

Can IP be presented positively? Yes, if you:

- Stress the value of the employees' own work. They are the ones producing and using the **information resources.** Put it on a personal basis. They are protecting their own end products and raw materials.
- Show how **control** can help productivity. For example, cleaning up a mess after a physical or logical disruption that could have been avoided or mitigated is not productive.
- Overcome preconceptions about overhead, bureaucracy, and "big brother."
- Deliver what you promise. Procedures must be rational. Technology must work. Administration must be active and even-handed.
- Motivate locally. Keeping top management and/or corporate staffs happy does not, by itself, strongly motivate users and local management over the long term. Self-motivation and peer example have staying power.

In the final analysis, the goal is for everyone to be his or her own security officer.

Managing a Crisis—or Keeping an Incident From Becoming One

16

Dealing With Hackers, Viruses, and Other Attacks

What's in this chapter?

- Hackers
- Viruses
- Other Attacks

This chapter examines the hacker, virus, and some other computer-related attacks as an issue for both enterprise and technical management. These attacks are literally capable of bringing an information processing system to a halt, destroying or hopelessly compromising software and data, or randomly affecting transactions and other processing activities. The more dependent an organization is on information processing, the more concerned management should be about susceptibility to attacks. At a rather early point in its development, consider making a formal review of your **information protection** (IP) program, looking both at **security** and **continuity** to determine that you are taking only appropriate attack-related risks. The discussion that follows is designed to help you develop such a review.

Hackers

The term *hacker* is ambiguous. It started out life innocuously enough by simply referring to people who knew their way around computer hardware and software. Someone who hacked around was a knowledgeable computer buff. Over time, the term came to be used for individuals who attacked other **systems,** seeking entry for malicious purposes. I suspect the transition came about as a result of some early computer buffs, dissatisfied with the hardware and software they had at their disposal, trying to play with the big kids' toys—that is, company-owned mainframes. I also suspect that what started out as technical curiosity turned into a ego-driven game.

Breaking into systems can get expensive if you have to do it by phone. So the most logical thing for attackers to do was to attempt to gain access to the long-distance telephone systems without paying. They did, and started to tell one another about it. This semiorganized attack on the phone system created a little more attention on the part of law enforcement. (Many of the attacks on individual computers were never reported.)

Some of these attackers were and are strongly antiestablishment. They see their role in life as bringing down the "institutions." Big business, government, and the phone companies all qualify for that title. Conveniently, those targets also have large hardware and software systems.

Not every hacker fits that profile. Some are just curious; some are just out for a lark. The problem is, you, as a manager, can't separate them, nor should you. You don't want any uninvited guests in your home, regardless of whether they came to trash the place or just look around. Entry is by invitation only.

Not all hackers come from the outside. You may find that some of your employees will try to hack from within. It's the same principle. The only difference is that your employees are probably more knowledgeable about where to go and what to look for. They may also have a more defined purpose in mind, like fraud or revenge.

Serious hackers with larceny in mind probably don't want you to know of their presence and will do a great deal to cover their electronic tracks. If your system is a way station to other systems, the idea is to keep things open. Here again, hackers will attempt to cover all their tracks so you won't close them out. On the other hand, a vengeful individual is happy only if you know what happened. Don't always expect hackers to leave you notes.

There are two basic steps hackers use to get where they want to go:

1. Find a hole in the access control system. They may try a variety of common passwords and weak passwords, intercept

a password, or use some of the setup passwords supplied by manufacturers to initialize or re-initialize systems (these last items should be erased immediately after use).
2. If Step 1 works, they try to take over the system. They try to become system administrators with all privileges, including granting and creating new privileges. From there on, they "own" the system. Privilege is the key to system hacking.

The questions of how many people have system control privileges, what they are permitted to do, and who watches over their shoulders are essential. If a hacker becomes one of these people, the first thing he or she may do is cancel everyone else's privileges. That pretty much makes the system the hacker's hostage. You may have to shut down and reconstruct the system.

This is why logging of access and checking the logs can be so important. It may be the only way you discover that some unusual access and privilege activity is going on. Some pretty sophisticated hackers have even developed techniques for tampering with logs, but not every hacker is a technical giant.

Here are some recommendations for dealing with hackers (some apply to you, some to technical management):

- Develop an authorization program. You can't control access unless you know what access privileges you want to grant and to whom.
- Install and enforce your access control software.
- Develop a program of password discipline or consider a one-time password system. One-time passwords make life very difficult for hackers.
- Limit the privileges any one individual can have and periodically check that those privileges are still intact. There are system software utility packages that do these things.
- Follow up on logs and report discrepancies.
- Treat hackers seriously. They are not something to tolerate. If you discover one on your system, you may wish to consider getting some professional help.

Should you report an attack to law-enforcement authorities? The most obvious answer is that if someone is violating the law and you know it, you should report it. The obvious answer is usually the best one, but there are some considerations that go with it. Will the authorities do anything? Tough to tell. Many police agencies still have no idea how to handle computer attacks. Some, unfortunately, don't take them seriously. The FBI usually gets involved if a federal law is violated. That usually means interstate activity, which is very probable. Don't get hung up on geography. Hackers don't. The odds are they have gained access to long-distance facilities and may be calling intercity, interstate, or internationally.

Should you prosecute? Don't waste the police's time if you don't intend to take the process to its conclusion. If they apprehend a hacker and you refuse to prosecute or supply evidence, you've actually strengthened the hacker's hand.

There may be reasons why you don't want to go public with the fact that a hacker is in your system. You may not wish to reveal your vulnerability until you've gotten rid of the weaknesses in your system. You may fear reprisal or destruction by the hacker. These are tough points to deal with generically. Each specific case has its own salient characteristics. However, try translating the attack into a physical context. Someone has broken into your offices or is holding an employee hostage. In that context, you may see a bit more clearly what you want to do.

Viruses

A virus is software that makes copies of itself and attempts to establish these copies in additional processing environments where more copies can be made and spread. It's a self-replicating vehicle that can carry different forms of attack or no attack at all. In its simplest form, by just replicating, the virus can chew up your storage and communications to the point where you can no longer use your system. In more advanced forms, not only does it replicate but it also brings a more specialized form of attack with it, such as formatting your hard disk or wiping out working storage.

Some viruses manifest themselves immediately. Others hide and appear after some type of trigger event, for example, a date, a given number of processing cycles, or the execution of a specific program.

Viruses appear much more often in personal computers (PCs) for a couple of good reasons: There are a lot more of them, and PC software usage is a much less controlled environment than that of mainframes. People buy or copy PC software from any number of sources; bulletin boards abound, attractive software (e.g., games) is primarily PC based; PCs are tied together much more loosely in networks. In short, software discipline on most PCs is woeful, and that is an open invitation for viruses to be introduced.

However, viruses are not always a PC-based phenomenon. They can be introduced at the mainframe or intermediate processor level directly or through other systems. Although many virus attacks have been directed at PCs or have entered a network through a PC to be uploaded or transmitted to other processors, PCs have no exclusive claim as virus origination points or targets. All processors are potentially vulnerable, directly or indirectly.

Also, although the more spectacular virus attacks have taken place within networks, viruses can do significant damage in a single processor. Think of a virus systematically attaching itself to a variety of programs in a system or **application** library or wiping storage devices clean on a single processor. If your systems are not networked, the possibility of a virus attack moving from one system to the next are obviously minimized. However, it is still possible to insert a virus into a single processor through job entry, system modification, or change management. Most viruses first enter PCs through diskettes, not over network lines.

All viruses do not necessarily come from the outside. Although dial-up facilities can certainly be a primary source of virus transmission, viruses can be inserted into a local area network (LAN), transaction or administrative network, or a single processor by anyone with access (authorized or otherwise).

Even though it requires a programmer to develop a virus, it doesn't require a programmer to spread one. Any individual who uses a system and has the right to enter software (or data that can be converted into executable form) can start a virus infection. Spreadsheet templates and utilities can be both virus sources and targets.

Viruses don't always advertise themselves. Anomalous behavior or results may be all you see, and these may not necessarily appear at the time of the attack. But not every anomaly is virus-originated. Virus paranoia, which can cause management to overly restrict the use of information system functions and connections or to pursue every unusual event as if it were a virus, can, in the long run, be more destructive than a real virus attack.

What has taken the virus out of the technical oddity category and put it squarely on the desks of concerned management is the dramatic growth of interconnection and transitivity on our information systems. (Transitivity simply means that software will run in many different processing domains.) Although viruses often make their first appearance through diskettes, networks certainly can help them spread. It's not uncommon for a virus to make its way around a LAN in short order and then to bridge from one LAN to the next. Given these two factors, it is possible for a single rogue program to transmit itself across thousands of nodes and then run in a large proportion of them. Although cutting back on *desired and authorized* connectivity and transitivity will cut back on virus susceptibility, it also has the unhappy effect of moving you backwards in productivity. This should be a solution of last resort.

However, *undesired and unauthorized* connections and compatibility are another matter. These can and should be controlled. But the protective groundwork has to be established first. Can you define your networks? This was easy enough to answer a few years ago, but not necessarily today. Consider how many modems and terminal emulators you have installed on PCs in your organization. To what can they connect? Are those same PCs part of LANs, and do they establish upstream and peer-to-peer connections such as workstations, remote job entry systems, or terminals? Do your LAN file servers have external connections? Are your networks interconnected through bridges or gateways to other external nets? Do you know the dimensions of those?

I've been asking these questions of clients and in every virus and network security session I attend. The answer is usually the same. They're not sure they can locate every connection.

Network protection is part of network management—both dawning arts. Implicit in being able to manage and protect networks is the ability to define their dimensions. This is a basic step that will help not only in antiviral situations but also in overall network management. Physical mapping as well as logical definition are necessary. A logical net is the connection you establish to carry out a particular set of applications. Think about it as if you were setting up conference calls. You use the same physical network facilities for all of them, but for each conference, you combine a different set of players. Information flows over the physical net in patterns established by the logical net. If you know the patterns, you can help control unwanted traffic, like viruses.

Conversely, if several different logical nets all pass through the same physical node or link, they will all be affected by an outage.

Many networks began life as relatively small, self-contained environments, and if security was designed into them at all, it was usually with that characteristic in mind. When two or more self-contained environments interconnect, the required security architecture becomes different. Now you must be aware of your external sources and determine under what conditions you should accept incoming traffic from each source. Conversely, you must be aware of what you are sending and the confidence you have in its integrity.

Most of the literature written about viruses speaks about the enterprise and its information systems as *victim*. Take a moment and consider your enterprise and its information systems as *transmitter*, direct or indirect. There are two general ways in which your organization can propagate viruses to other enterprises. One is through internetwork connections; the other is through the supply of software (or data) in which unwanted executable code (that is, viruses) can be embedded. Bulletin boards, freeware, and shrink-wrapped packaged software from vendors are not the only sources of program transfer. Many organizations today conduct data and transaction interchanges with processing partners—electronic funds transfer; cash management; electronic data interchange for manufacturing, process, or distribution industries; reservation systems; point of sale; insurance agency systems; academic and research systems.

To enable these partners to participate fully in the exchange, the originating organizations often supply them with software to handle transactions and data. Do you distribute software? Inside your enterprise to departments and subsidiaries? Outside your enterprise to processing partners?

As part of your management review of virus susceptibility, make sure you review any ways in which you may be, unwittingly, the cause of a virus attack on some other organization. Most organizations don't spend much time discussing *mutual* security obligations when they decide to interconnect or pass on software. Such agreements should be mandatory before beginning interchange.

I have often wondered how much time is spent in merger and acquisition negotiations discussing the compatibility of information processing between the joining enterprises. And how much of that discussion centers around mutual information protection? I suspect very little or none at all. For that matter, in a divestiture, is attention paid to what connections may still be left in the severed organization that could let the divested enterprise reenter your systems?

Do you know where your software is coming from, and can you develop a level of assurance about what your suppliers are doing to protect you? This is not an easy task. First, you must have a good idea of what software is being used in your enterprise and where it's coming from. In an ocean of PCs, workstations, and miniprocessors, getting an inventory of the software in use calls for a very comprehensive review and the cooperation of everyone involved. You can probably scale this effort down significantly by concentrating only on those processors and systems that are critical from a confidentiality or availability standpoint. Even this can be a large job. The alternative is to put the responsibility on local management to ensure that software discipline is in place. This isn't impossible, and depending on how it's done, it can be quite effective.

There are several other issues related to viruses:

• *Education.* How do you raise the knowledge level of the technical, management, and user communities about the nature and effect of viruses? Unless all of your information-using community has an appreciation for a virus's impact, can recognize the symptoms, and know the first steps to be performed if they suspect a virus, a lot of damage can occur before it's stopped. A state of virus paranoia can also be created, causing every anomaly and failure to be reported as a virus. Your virus awareness program should address the issue at two levels:

1. A general review of virus characteristics, their impact, and steps to be followed for the nontechnical management and user groups.
2. A more in-depth familiarization of virus behavior and symptoms for those members of the technical community who will have responsibility for developing preventive and response programs. This should include telecommunications specialists as well as technically competent PC and workstation users.

• *Planning.* What action plans and programs do you need to prevent and deal with virus infections? A full-scale antiviral program beginning with an analysis of susceptibility and ending with tested action programs for an entire enterprise can be a lengthy and costly affair, depending on the existing level of security and contingency activity. In some organizations, this could represent the first comprehensive, enterprise-wide information protection program initiated. This is especially true of those organizations that have put their security emphasis on mainframe system and application protection.

To keep the direct and indirect costs of an antiviral program within practical limits, it may be necessary to prioritize those environments and applications that are considered critical to the ongoing operation of the organization and determine what processing links are the most likely avenues for virus attack. Although this is not necessarily the optimum technical solution, it may be the only viable approach for an initial effort.

It's better to expend some effort in this direction and reduce the threat than to develop a plan that has no chance of financial acceptance. However, a reduced-scope plan must be recognized by senior management and all concerned individuals as exactly that—an incomplete plan. Proposals for future follow-on activities should be submitted along with the initial plan to prevent misunderstanding that the first phase is the complete program.

Inject as much reality as you can into the process. Don't consider convoluted attacks that depend on the conjunction of a series of unlikely circumstances. Concentrate on disposing of the more likely threats. Determining what these threats are should involve all the concerned parties, not just the technicians. If you think an inventory of software and software sources is required, measure this, too, in practical terms and think about doing it in phases.

• *Control.* How do you establish ground rules for controlling the entry and use of executable software into systems and applications in a practical and cost-effective manner? On the basis of the planning done in the preceding step, a series of control processes and ground rules should be established for access control, software introduction and verification, backup integrity, process isolation, and limits to connectivity and transitivity, if any.

This is where reality checks are extremely important. Can the control process you've developed be realistically implemented and enforced? If not, don't even try for management approval. Go back to the drawing board.

• *Identification.* An anomaly has occurred. Is this a virus? Some other attack? If it is a virus, can you recognize its nature and recommend an appropriate response? This process has at least two levels. Initial recognition of a possible virus should be accomplished by the first person to notice an irregularity. This could be anyone in the information processing system, so this skill should be imparted to all players.

A second level of virus diagnosis is best carried out by technically skilled individuals within reasonable proximity of the affected systems. Timing can be key in detecting and limiting a virus. Appointing one or two people within an enterprise to develop these skills may sound like a good distribution of labor for an event of unknown probability, but the number of people should be determined by the number of distinct processing environments there are and the speed with which these individuals can respond. If your company spans time zones, you should probably consider creating a hot-line service.

Do antiviral software packages work? Yes, but be sure you know what they are intended to do. Virus scanners look for known viruses or the known characteristics of viruses. They will not stop a brand new breed.

Inoculation programs do something different. They act as an authentication mechanism for existing software. By inoculating a piece of software, you take a total of the bits and their value in the program and attach some form of coded or encrypted message to the end of the package. If anything attaches itself to the software, you'll know it because you check the program against the coded verification "stub" each time it runs. Any discrepancy and you have a good indication that the program has been altered, perhaps by a virus tagging on, perhaps by other causes.

• *Response.* Can you isolate the infected system? Track where the infection has been? Stop the spread? Can you keep your systems and applications running while you do? The first order of business after a *potential* virus has been discovered is limiting its impact. Even if a virus has not been determined for sure, if the environment requires it, isolate the suspect system. If you want to test for a virus, don't transport the suspicious software to another system unless that system has been prepared for a virus test. That requires full and verified isolation of the test system under controlled procedures. This same principle applies to both PCs and mainframes. If you're not careful, your response and reconstruction processes can easily become vehicles for continuing the spread of the virus.

• *Reconstruction.* How do you get data, programs, and systems operational again without reintroducing the virus? How do you rebuild clean databases and system/application libraries? You should withstand the temptation to rebuild too soon. Bringing an isolated system back up and on-line or restoring files before determining whether the backup copies are also compromised could reintroduce the virus and destroy any chance of full reconstruction and recovery.

In dealing with viruses, backup is a mixed bag. Making copies of already infected programs and reintroducing them into your computer after you've gotten rid of the first copy can be a real exercise in frustration. A safer ploy is to back up your *data* only. Keep original copies of your software locked away. Use the originals, which you can be reasonably sure were not infected, to restart the system.

• *Review.* Can you determine how the virus was introduced and track back to its entry point? Make a full analysis of the events, symptoms, diagnosis, and steps taken by representatives of all the groups involved as rapidly as possible. This is key to determining whether any residual effects or copies of the virus still exist and for shutting down the most probable paths of entry. Make an effort to get an intact copy of the virus for identification and analysis. This may not always be possible. The replicated and propagated versions may not look the same as the original, since self-modification as well as host modification is a characteristic of many virus programs.

Some viruses self-destruct after execution. Nevertheless, unless you carry out a review, you can't be confident that the attack is really over. Even after a thorough post-analysis, your confidence may not be total.

The management program I've outlined is certainly not a cure-all for the virus threat. We're still learning about these things. However, I hope it has helped to put the virus in better perspective, provided some useful advice to better protect against virus attack, and laid the groundwork for a program to deal with an actual virus. Let's hope you never have to use it.

Other Attacks

There are a couple of other kinds of attacks we should discuss (besides the obvious ones like someone taking a hatchet to a machine or bringing a bomb into a data center).

Logic bombs are programs that are written to do damage when a certain set of circumstances arises. Viruses are programs that replicate and can act as vehicles for other forms of attack—the logic bomb is one of them. However, a logic bomb doesn't need a virus to get where it's going. It can be planted directly by a knowledgeable programmer or systems operator.

The best defense against a logic bomb is generic, since it may sit for long periods before the trigger circumstances occur. The Friday the thirteenth attack was a logic bomb—set to go off when system calendars changed to Friday the thirteenth. Since you don't know what form one of these things will take, the safest course is control of software. Permit only authorized copies of authorized software to be deployed on a system. Make sure at least two people are involved in the deployment. If this is too difficult for the entire enterprise, cut the process back to critical systems, but do it.

Trojan horses are programs that look like one thing but do another. Games and utilities are the most likely source, such as a new whiz-bang piece of software that creates psychedelic images on your screen while it's systematically wiping out your hard disk. The same countermeasures apply. Know your software sources; check out the software before using it on a production machine; authorize it for use; enforce the use of authorized-only software.

17

Dealing With Computer Fraud, Disclosure, Espionage, and Illegal Copies

---

What's in this chapter?

- Computer Fraud
- Disclosure and Espionage
- Illegal Copies

This chapter covers some of the other unpleasant incidents that can come your way through the use of information processing systems.

Computer Fraud

What makes computer fraud different from other forms of fraud? Fundamentally, nothing. Someone is still trying to reap ill-gotten gains by misrepresentation. The difference is in technique.

Oddly enough, general experience tells us that most computer frauds take place because an individual has discovered a weakness in controls and finally succumbs to the temptation to capitalize on that weakness. I'm sure there have been well-planned, deliberate fraudulent attacks on information **systems** by criminal masterminds, but mostly we see hands stuck in the electronic equivalent of a cookie jar.

Who commits most of these crimes? Whenever the subject of computer fraud comes up, the first group that gets the suspicious eye is the programmers, especially the systems programmers. Aren't they the guys who can change the code around to suit their own purposes? True, but they also have to be in a position to direct the results of their misdeeds to their own advantage. That usually means some operating access to the system. If they design a fraudulent process into the **application** but never get a chance to use it, what good does it do them? Most fraud is perpetrated by users and others with applications access.

There are several different types of fraud. The simplest involves just changing a value in a record: Credit ratings, final exam grades, employment records, medical records, and Social Security records can all be altered. The cheater just changes the data, and the system does the rest.

There are more involved forms of fraud such as creating payments to a nonexistent company. This involves creating a whole series of supporting files and transactions to make the phantom look real. The checks that are issued have to be handled carefully so they cannot be traced back to the source.

One approach that always gets a mention because of its colorful name is the "salami" technique. This is the accounting classic of altering the roundup function in calculations of interest or other forms of payments due to an account. Instead of rounding up to the next cent or dollar, salami artists cut off the process and take the rounding results and put them into special accounts they have created. Cent by cent, done over a couple of hundred thousand accounts per period, it adds up. There are other forms of low-level, cumulative cheating that can add up to a pile of money.

To make any of these things happen, the accounting as well as the **security** controls have to be loose. Obviously the individual has to be in a position of unchallenged control or must have an understanding of what the controls will detect and won't. The basics of authorization, access control, separation of duties, audit trails, and enforcement all apply here. There's no magic.

One thing to look at in your applications are the so-called default options in transaction menus. *Default* as it's used here doesn't refer to financial default. It's the process that takes place if you don't choose any of the alternatives presented or select an undesignated option. (Let's say you're presented options numbered 1 through 8. What happens if you key in a 9?) Sometimes these open-ended options allow a knowledgeable individual to create his or her own transactions. All menus as they appear to the user should be closed-ended.

One other area to tighten up on is application testing. When a piece of software is presented for deployment, it should have undergone independently verified testing of not only the mainstream functions but the odd combinations as well. Letting programmers design their own tests without supervision or any standards is an open invitation to weak controls. The programmer may not be dishonest, but there may be anomalies lurking in the application waiting for someone to discover them.

How does it happen that bugs appear in programs two or three years after they've been deployed? It's probably the first time the peculiar set of circumstances that triggered the bug arose. Obviously, they were not encountered in testing. Another scenario is that the bug was created as a result of changes introduced into the system. That's why regression testing is so important. Not only should the change be tested, but all the other functions should be retested to ensure that the new code hasn't affected anything else. Do most organizations do it? Not as thoroughly as they should.

Disclosure and Espionage

Whenever you come across discussions on threats to computer security, disclosure gets the lion's share of the attention, although most organizations put disruption first on their lists of worries. Why? I think it goes back to the major concerns about privacy that raged around computers in the 1980s (see Chapter 19). Coupled with this concern is the almost insatiable appetite that Americans (and others) seem to have for high-tech spy stories.

I am not minimizing the potential damage of or susceptibility to disclosure. It's a real threat. But it's not the only threat.

The real question about disclosure is whether the computer is the primary source of vulnerability. In many cases, it's easier to bribe someone, go through the paper trash, or walk into an office than to try and break into a computer or intercept telecommunications.

There are two basic forms of disclosure-related attacks: passive and active. The passive form of interception cuts into a communications process and picks up whatever is coming across. Such things as satellite or microwave pickups, bugs, or telephone taps are the most common. Generally you don't know they are there, although there are ways of detecting taps.

You may have noticed a flurry of articles on "computer emanations" back in the late 1980s. It was proven that some terminals and personal computers (PCs), under the proper circumstances, emit radio signals that contain intelligible information. It was further demonstrated that with a relatively small investment in equipment, a rather strong sense of determination, and a lot of time, an individual could pick up from a reasonable distance what was appearing on a terminal screen or passing through a system. What was passing through a system wasn't much help because its passage was so swift. But an image stays on a screen for longer periods of time and is refreshed by the display circuitry. That could be a source of information.

It was an interesting exercise, and it did cause manufacturers to redesign displays to reduce emanation. A military set of standards for emanation-resistant systems already existed under the code name "Tempest." The other interesting thing is that there were practically no known cases of the attack actually taking place. Granted, with that sort of attack you probably don't know it's happening. However, if someone gets and uses valuable information to your detriment, you usually see the aftereffects.

I suspect that the reason for such few attacks had to do with the randomness of the information available. To get something really useful from an attack, attackers have to know exactly what they are looking for, where it is, and when it will be available. It also has to appear in a usable form. Most of those elements are missing from a passive attack. Essentially, attackers are shopping and playing the odds that something valuable will come to the surface.

Since, in dealing with passive attacks, you don't know about a specific opponent or attack to defend against, generic defenses are best, especially encryption. If you encrypt what you don't want the opponent to see, it doesn't matter whether it's captured or not. It's useless unless it can be decrypted. Unfortunately, screen emanations are an exception.

Active attacks are different. It may be a browser who is just looking for something interesting, but the other type of active attack is more worrisome. Here the individual knows what to look for, knows how to find it, knows when it will be available, and probably can make sense of it. Often this type of attacker is an insider. Access control and encryption both help in these cases.

The need-to-know principle gets dragged out for discussion in these circumstances. If you have a very well structured classification system such as the military uses and *people as well as information are classified*, need to know can be made effective, but most organizations do not classify their people by giving them clearances. In some cases, even with a category clearance such as "Top Secret," you still need to be cleared for that specific file or data element. Even fewer organizations do that. You can control who can read or modify information on a computer system through the rules processing of the access control software. What usually stops need to know is the process of actually authorizing individuals. That's a management process, and it gets ticklish.

It's difficult to challenge someone who says, "I need this information to do my job." It has all sorts of political and bureaucratic overtones that may run contrary to the culture of the enterprise. Don't wave around need to know unless you know you can pull it off. If you do use it, start with a small number of files and individuals.

Suppose you do get a case of unauthorized disclosure. What you do depends on the actual situation and how you discovered it. Being told a file is being held for ransom and all your copies are gone is a combination of disclosure and disruption with a strong dose of extortion mixed in. Seeing your new designs in a trade journal may be a bit different from getting a call from a competitor who says he was just offered your client lists. Each one involves special, on-the-spot, treatment.

There are some general points to be made, however:

- Close off the source as soon as you can. It sounds basic, but I have seen instances in which organizations were so intent on tracking down the culprit that they never closed the barn door. If the data are there, protect them.
- Get some professional help. Leave the detective work to people who know how to handle it.
- Don't do anything illegal or embarrassing. False accusations, invading an individual's privacy, and jumping to conclusions can do more damage than the loss of the data.
- After the event, analyze in detail how it happened and review your security process. Don't overreact or start a reign of terror. Tighten things up, but do it in a way that will not create serious morale problems.

Illegal Copies

The whole issue of illegal copies boils down to understanding what you are authorized or not authorized to do. The most common instance of illegal copying is software, but there are other cases, such as proprietary files, that are equally important. If you subscribe to an information service on-line, it is probably pretty careful about protecting its data. If you download data from that service, check your contract with the servicer before you distribute it to all comers. Usage may be restricted to you and you alone.

If the data or software is distributed through diskettes or optical disks, once again, check your authorization. Most people don't understand or don't care to understand that they have purchased a license to use the material under certain circumstances. They have not purchased the materials themselves. Legally, it is not your software, and you can't do what you like with it. The concept of licensed usage is neither intuitively obvious nor particularly comfortable to most people. It's another one of those "unnatural acts." If you think trying to control making copies of documents is tough, controlling software and electronic data copying is even tougher.

There have been technological techniques such as copy protection used in the past, but that raised all sorts of problems with the use of hard disks in computers or making backups. Most software today is unprotected. However, the manufacturers have not given up their data rights in the process.

One last thought to round out this chapter: Are you a software supplier? I know you're not LOTUS or Microsoft, but you'd be surprised at the number of companies that supply software internally to their customers or vendors to make it easier to do business with them. Do you distribute software either outside or inside your enterprise?

If you do, is everything you're distributing yours to distribute? Have you included some vendor's software in the package you sent out that you had no right to send without special permission from the vendor? What controls do you need over the software you distribute? Is it OK for your software recipients to make copies (and modifications) without your approval? If not, what have you done to control the situation?

I hope you now have a little more insight into some of the subtleties that can arise out of computer incidents. Your management skills and sensitivities are more important in preventing and handling incidents than all of the technical processes.

18

Dealing With External Entities

You are not in the **information protection** (IP) process alone. Neither is your organization. Wherever your information **systems** go and wherever **information** about you goes, your information protection concerns should go too. Spend a little time thinking through some of the relationships your organization has and the impact information has on them.

Law Enforcement

You will probably encounter some wide variations in skill and interest in computer crime among the law-enforcement groups you deal with. There are some plausible (if not good) reasons for this. Most law-enforcement agencies are under pretty tight budget constraints these days. Training or hiring computer specialists for anything besides their own information processing needs is tough to justify. In the face of requirements for more drug, rape, robbery, assault, and murder protection, computer crime has a pretty low priority.

In addition, computer crime law is not always easy to understand or prosecute. Many district attorneys shy away from it for this reason. They are not the easiest cases in the world to present; most juries don't understand computer crime, and the judge may be in the same boat. Gathering evidence and keeping it untainted is no small job.

Jurisdictional disputes arise very readily in IP-related crimes, especially because of networks. The victim may be in one city, the perpetrator in another, and the actual processing that caused the incident in a third. It may even involve different countries.

Finally, the small number of people or organizations that have shown themselves willing to prosecute when an incident has occurred only discourages law-enforcement groups that are interested in pursuing computer-related crimes.

Does this mean that legal recourse is a joke? No. There is a building history of case law about this subject. It's growing slowly, but it's growing. The press brings the issue back to the front pages periodically, and law enforcement does respond to the press. You can help by participating in or even sponsoring programs on the subject of computer-related crimes and soliciting help from the private sector in setting forth its expectations from law enforcement and vice versa.

The Press

If a serious incident occurs in your company or to someone else in your city or industry, be prepared. The odds are pretty good you'll get a call from the press.

There are a number of professionals who provide excellent advice and training for executives in how to work with the press. This kind of training is necessary for anyone who could end up dealing with the media, regardless of subject or position.

These are a few basics: Get your story straight before the media get to you. This doesn't mean you should lie; lying to the press can produce much worse results than telling the truth. Just assemble what you really know and talk it through with someone else, especially your press relations people. Keep it simple and factual; don't embellish or speculate. Keep the jargon to a minimum. The reporter will interpret the jargon according to his or her own knowledge, and you may not like the results. Try not to sound defensive. Defensiveness implies you're holding something back. Think of everything you say as if it were a banner headline or the opening clip on the six o'clock news. Don't make sensational statements; on the other hand, under no circumstances say "No comment." That is tantamount to admitting some fault or guilt.

What reporters say to you and what they write are two different things. They may seem totally sympathetic to your plight, and then lay you out on page one.

Also important is how your management reacts to the press. Some organizations believe that any publicity is bad publicity; some believe just the opposite. If you believe your management is going to overreact negatively, make sure you have a witness or a recording of everything you say to the press. Having a third party present is always a good idea anyway. If you get a phone inquiry, try to arrange to call the reporter back; in the meantime, get your act together.

Regulators

If you are in a regulated industry, the unannounced arrival of investigating teams is not out of the question. Often there is a solid reason for the investigation, so don't get too defensive. The same applies to criminal or civil investigations.

The point to remember is that you still have your rights as an individual and as a manager. Get identification. Let your management know they are there. Get assistance from the legal department and other appropriate sources. Do not let anyone near your terminals or equipment unless you are in control of the activities. Regulators and law-enforcement officers have rights, but the days of the Spanish Inquisition are gone.

Keep a record of what they ask for and do. Be careful to check that all data returned to you are the same as when you turned them over. If they make copies, know what they copied.

The process need not be hostile. It's probably better for you if it isn't. But keep in mind that these are outsiders (a special class of outsider, to be sure), and you should not relax your control over them any more than you would anyone else. In fact, managers have been written up for being too liberal in what they would allow the investigators to see or do in an uncontrolled fashion.

Regulators' reports are usually a matter of public record. If they are going to investigate proprietary material, get the legal department involved before—not after—they get the materials. Otherwise, your strategic plans may be open to public scrutiny.

The Public

The first consideration is the information you voluntarily tell the public. If your organization deals heavily in public trust, such as a financial institution or an airline, you may want to take the initiative and publish your security policy, privacy protection activities, and concern for confidentiality. If you are in a dangerous industry, such as one involving toxic substances or radioactive power, you might want to include your computer- and network-related safety measures in any materials you distribute.

There is plenty of public relations value to be gotten from an intelligent publication of your security policies and objectives. However, you do not want to publish the specifics of your program for any potential attacker to see.

The second consideration is the reactive release of information in response to requests, ranging from the concerned citizen to an advocacy group. Most of what I said about the press also applies here, only more so.

A reporter may or may not have a bias, but the odds are extremely good that the members of the public who approach you have a very significant bias, and it's seldom in your favor. They may often have a hidden agenda as well. Once again, get help. Remember, too, that they probably share neither your knowledge nor your positive feelings about information processing.

You are usually under no obligation to respond to most questions about your **security** or **continuity** measures. Freedom of information usually doesn't extend that far. But think twice about stonewalling; the result may be increased hostility. Try to cooperate, but on your terms.

Vendors and Processing Partners

Your vendors and processing partners are important and should be included in all of your IP considerations. The IP world doesn't end at the walls of your enterprise. Start putting more of your IP relations with others in writing. The only way you are going to be able to conduct an orderly and effective IP program that involves other entities is by imposing a certain level of formality on the process. The way to get this going is to volunteer your side of the agreement first: Here's what we are going to do to protect you. Now, what are you going to do to protect us? Most vendors live in a world of nondisclosure agreements. That's not a bad place to start discussions on IP.

If you use service bureaus, systems integrators, contract programmers, software suppliers, hardware suppliers and service groups, telecommunications supply and maintenance companies, or consultants, part of your agreement with them should cover the protective measures you will mutually employ in the areas of service they supply. You may want to run checks on some of their people who will be resident and determine whether they are adequately bonded. Don't rely on your company's standard agreements. You are in a special situation, and your security requirements should be reflected in that agreement.

Customers and Shareholders

Customers and shareholders are the external groups you most want to keep happy. Protect your customers as if they were part of your business. Some managers might react negatively to that, but think about it. Your customers are an important part of your business; let them know what you are doing to protect them as part of the added value that comes from doing business with you. Solicit their comments and requirements. Make your sales and customer service forces aware of what you're doing. Most salespeople will figure out a way to capitalize on it.

Your shareholders, at least the ones that read any of the material your company sends out, are always looking for signs of good management. Although the performance of the stock and the size of the dividend are the major indicators from their standpoint, there are other items that are interesting—new products, new ventures, expansion, new uses of technology. In all of these categories, even a short sentence in the middle of a product description about how your company protects its proprietary information can get you some mileage. You might as well; you'll get the criticism soon enough if anything goes wrong. It won't cure your problems, but a file full of positive statements issued in the past may help you ride out some of the problems of the present or future.

The Changing World of Information Processing

19

Laws, Regulations, and Compliance

What's in this chapter?

- Personal Privacy
- Computer Crime
- Occupational Safety and Health
- Fair Credit and Fair Employment Practices
- Copyright and Intellectual Property
- Telecommunications Law
- Libel, Defamation, and Freedom of Speech
- Insider Trading and Information

This is not legal or regulatory advice. It is a collection of observations from an individual who has had experience and contact with the subjects over the years. No more, no less.

This chapter is intended to raise your awareness on the number and types of new legal and regulatory areas related to **information protection** (IP) and to provide a little assistance in sorting them out. For those areas that are of prime concern to you and your company, get some specific advice from a legal or regulatory specialist. Your internal legal staff or external law firm may not always be familiar with all of the branches of law being discussed here, so don't expect immediate and clear-cut responses to your first inquiries. LEXIS and WESTLAW are two legal query systems you may wish to become familiar with.

A wide variety of local, state, provincial, national, and international laws, standards, and agreements have been passed relating to **information** and **information resources.** Their enforcement is, at best, variable. The subject areas include:

- Personal privacy
- Computer crime
- National security
- Environmental protection
- Occupational safety and health
- Fair credit practices
- Fair employment practices and labor relations
- Copyright and intellectual property rights
- Telecommunications law
- Libel and defamation
- Freedom of information
- Freedom of speech
- Financial disclosure and generally accepted accounting principles
- Insider trading and other securities regulations

There is a vast array of specific regulations covering individual industries such as medicine, public utilities, banking, brokerage, transportation, manufacturing, and retail. Some of the rules specifically address information and information resources; others get there by indirection. They all can have an impact on your assignment.

A few items on the list can have interesting implications.

Personal Privacy

Personal privacy gets a lot of attention. The prospect of some giant organization keeping minutely detailed files on our comings and goings is good for at least a dozen stories, films, or exposés a year. Some are quite accurate; others are farfetched. There are three major points relating to personal privacy:

1. *Individuals have the right to see information about themselves.* Through a variety of channels, ranging from freedom of information to fair credit or fair employment, individuals determined to get at records about themselves have a pretty good arsenal of weapons to use. Few people actually exercise this right, but if you get such a request, don't dismiss it out of hand simply because the company has never done it before. Don't roll right over and comply either. Get an opinion on what your company's and the individual's rights are. Get that opinion in specific terms related to the information requested.

There could well be special rules in your state or community dealing with credit; background checks; criminal records; medical

documents; political, social, and labor affiliations; job performance; accident reports; and even such things as marital status and school transcripts.

It's interesting how few people really exercise their rights relative to this legislation. Don't let that lull you into inattention. The excuse that no one has used the power of the law previously has little standing if you're in violation.

These rules may sometimes vary from community to community, especially in large cities, but the major source of variability will be at the state or, in Canada, provincial level.

Get an understanding of the applicable venue or venues in which the request is being made. Depending on the way the law is written, where the information is actually physically stored may make a difference. Is the venue where the data are stored, where they appear, or the home of the enterprise that owns the data? If there are multiple copies, which location applies? Are you allowed to keep multiple copies? It may not matter, or it may be critical.

The odds are that you or the information seeker will run afoul of some technicality for which there are conflicting interpretations. Most of this legislation and regulatory content was written broadly, often in the context of a technology that is now obsolete and without much in the way of precedent to help it along. When many of the laws currently in force were first written, the personal computer (PC), local area network (LAN), and distributed database, for example, were unknown concepts. Not all the legislation has been updated to reflect some of the practical changes these technologies introduced.

If a service bureau is holding and processing the information on your behalf, that usually doesn't get you off the hook.

2. *The concept of "person" varies around the world.* A concept that caused a major to-do in the 1980s between European and U.S. privacy experts was the natural person versus the legal person. In a nutshell, you and I are natural persons; companies are legal persons. A number of European countries grant the same privacy rights to a legal person as they do a natural person. The argument was about the right of one company to find out what another company knew or said about it—such as credit performance or competitive weaknesses. It was also about whether contractual agreements and laws affecting business relations made the legal person concept unnecessary or actually conflicted with it.

The legal person exists as a privacy consideration in some European countries and a few other places throughout the world. There were relatively few actual cases heard and adjudicated on the principle (at least to date); if you deal with overseas entities or have information resources, electronic or otherwise, be aware that one person's company may be another person's person.

3. *The role of government in privacy concerns.* In the United States, government is often considered the most likely offender, and much of the legislation, especially that written at the federal level, is geared toward reining in the rights of government agencies such as the IRS, immigration, the FBI, and others.

In other countries, privacy legislation regards the private sector as the ogre and the government as the protector of the people. In fact, the government may even be the keeper of the critical information it does not want the private sector to hold itself. The point is, don't take U.S. assumptions with you when you look at foreign information-related legislation and regulations.

The enforcement structures are also different. Frequently, in Europe you'll find an Information Privacy Directorate, Inspectorate, or similar name.

Computer Crime

The definition of computer crime varies widely from state to state. Law enforcement—how and by whom—also varies. Is hacking a felony, a misdemeanor, or a crime at all? What constitutes hacking? There are major differences in definitions and penalties around the United States. The virus is another issue that is still being clarified legally. The trial of Robert Morris in 1990 helped to straighten out some issues, but it left others untouched.

In some states, using a computer to defraud or commit other crimes may make it special type of violation. There are certain computer crimes that are singled out by federal legislation, primarily attacks on or misuse of government-owned systems. The banking system also gets special treatment in the same federal statutes.

Another legal issue is, what is a computer as it relates to computer crime? Legislative experts have had a field day with this one. In an effort to exclude things such as hand-held calculators or toys with microprocessors, some of the definitions get remarkably technical and fine-lined in their distinctions. The only trouble is that the technology keeps changing and refuses to stay legally defined. The personal computer is usually covered, although someone may try to exclude a portable simply because it is portable or hand-held.

Telecommunications networks can also be the subject of a different form of dispute. Does computer crime apply to the network as well as the processors, or are the laws about misuse of telecommunications facilities involved? Most LANs would be considered processors, and many people try to make the distinction between public and private telecommunications, but even that doesn't break evenly.

The law *as written* often will not be your first line of practical understanding of what is or is not criminal activity. You're going to need case law and judicial interpretations to make any real sense out of some of the situations.

I think we can handle *national security* with a single comment. The Departments of Defense and Energy as well as the various intelligence and criminal justice units have very specific rules about the handling of classified information. Follow them.

Environmental protection is primarily concerned with potentially toxic substances used in the building of or disposal of used computing equipment. There are few, if any, computer-specific items that a user has to worry about. Some manufacturers from time to time have had problems with chemicals used in chip or media production. Disposal of supplies may also be subject to certain recycling regulations.

Occupational Safety and Health

There are two major occupational safety and health concerns, neither of which is settled at the time of this writing. One is the effect of radiation (emanations) from display screens. The other has to do with the effect that use of computer keyboards for sustained periods of time can have on the wrists, lower arms, and elbows. There have been a number of research studies done on both of these issues and several lawsuits. Supporting evidence has landed on both sides of the issue.

Another item of concern is the general working conditions under which operators perform their duties, including lighting, proper chairs and desks, sufficient breaks and rest periods, and freedom from hazards such as surface-running cables or projections.

Fair Credit and Fair Employment Practices

Most fair credit and fair employment laws are variations on the privacy theme. However, there is also a major **security** issue. It involves not only the information you know about someone, but also what steps you are taking to protect that information from disclosure and misuse. It's the classic combination of privacy and security, backed up by regulatory as well as fiduciary responsibilities.

Operator monitoring—using the computer itself to monitor and report on individual performance—is one such issue. This has been the subject of labor disputes, regulations, and lawsuits. Generally, monitoring as a process has not fared well. One special case illustrates the kinds of problems you can have because the law isn't necessarily consistent.

In Italy, there is a legal requirement to use security measures for certain classes of confidential or important financial data. The use of an access control mechanism, which, in addition to granting or refusing access, also logs the user on and off and keeps an audit trail for tracing violations, is strongly recommended if not mandated. An Italian labor union interpreted a law forbidding monitoring of employees to include the use of access control systems and sued. (The law was written primarily against clandestine spying, hidden cameras, and the like). The suit went on for a long time and was finally settled by placing severe restrictions on who could have access to the logs of the access control facility and under what circumstances the logs could be used. By trying to obey one law, you could violate another.

Copyright and Intellectual Property

It is not enough to declare a piece of information proprietary. You must behave, yourself, as if you believed it. Several disclosure cases have been thrown out of court or the sanctions vastly reduced because the defendant showed that, in spite of declarations of trade secrecy or proprietary ownership, the organization normally did not act in an appropriately protective manner toward the data. In short, it's not just what you say, it's what you do.

Software copying is a violation of copyright law. Even if you've published pamphlets and posters about it, if your people are still doing it, you could be liable. Again, it's what your organization does, not what it's management says it does. Note, however, that being in actual violation and not having issued any management guidance at all is worse than being in violation in spite of your guidance to the contrary.

Telecommunications Law

Telecommunications law covers a wide range of areas from disruption through use of telecomms for illegal purposes. Theft of service is a common item with hackers, who use corporate telephone cards and facilities for their long-distance sorties. There are rules about illegal or unauthorized hookups that are somewhat more complicated overseas, especially in those countries where the Postal Telephone and Telegraph (PTT) authorities are government-owned monopolies. Americans who are now used to hooking up practically anything to anything and having a choice of services to use in the process are sometimes dismayed when they find restrictions in many European countries concerning what you can attach to a line and who can attach it. In several countries, if you communicate over it, the PTT owns it and controls it.

Libel, Defamation, and Freedom of Speech

Information systems are tools that can be involved, with their managers, in disputes having to do with access, use of information, and the circumstances under which they can be used. Computer-based bulletin boards have been the subject of freedom of speech as well as libel and defamation proceedings based on the types of information that was being stored and communicated by bulletin board subscribers. Was the bulletin board operator responsible? Did the operator have the right to monitor and censor the information on the boards, even if it was criminal, such as transmitting active credit-card numbers for use by potential hackers? Most of the conclusions so far have been case-specific. The issue is not clearly defined.

Insider Trading and Information

Because of the wide range of information and information services available to employees and others dealing with an enterprise, the potential for individuals to obtain insider information through poorly protected systems is great.

Don't become paranoid about the legal or regulatory environment. It is a real, but practical, business-oriented approach that applies to IP as it does everywhere else.

20

The Future of Information Protection

Making predictions about **information protection** (IP) means making predictions about information processing. To do that, the usual procedure calls for building on assumptions about technological progress. It's no secret that technology has been a major enabling force for a vast number of social, political, and economic phenomena over the past century and that developments in information usage have benefited greatly from this technical ground swell. But I suspect that by concentrating exclusively on the technology, we may underestimate the human component.

Some technologies arrive at exactly the right time to fulfill the pent-up needs of a large population of potential users (the copy machine and the mainframe computer). Other entries are attractive enough, or improve the current technology sufficiently, to create a strong desire that ultimately translates into a need (the personal computer, the fax machine, the desktop laser printer, and the compact disk). Others just don't make it (the talking car that would remind you that "your door is ajar").

In each instance, some degree of personal, social, or organizational readiness was required for the technology to catch on. If the user community doesn't see a need or, at least, a level of usefulness or attractiveness, nothing will happen. The threshold of acceptance is, of course, highly dependent on many other things, such as price, ease of use, reliability, common interfaces, and, at least initially, some degree of novelty.

Generally speaking, until now, **security** has been something of an afterthought as a condition for accepting a technology. Is that attitude changing? Somewhat, but not fast enough to keep up.

Let's examine some of the possible areas of change in the use of information resources over the next four or five years. I restrict the discussion to areas that have these three characteristics:

1. A feasible technology is or will probably be available. By feasible, I mean that it works and you won't need an advanced degree to use it. It can become commonly available at a reasonable price, and the cost of entry is not extreme (e.g., you don't have to throw everything out and start again—such as a totally incompatible TV broadcast standard).

2. A sufficiently strong need or desire will probably exist within a large enough population to make the change worth considering.

3. Some **control,** security, or **continuity** issues will result that are worth our attention.

Information on Demand Through Location- and Device-Independent Access to Data

In the period up to the early 1980s, there was a very strong bond between the data and where they were physically stored. If you wanted specific **information,** you went to a specific file cabinet, a specific file, a specific document, page, line, and perhaps even word. The same process held true with computers. Data could be found on a specific disk or tape that was attached or attachable to a specific computer. You needed fairly clear knowledge of the physical location to find the data you wanted.

Then along came databases, especially relational databases, and physical location has been slowly replaced by "views"—a way of describing the data you want without reference to physical location or processing facility. The end result is that information can be called up by a user who has no knowledge of its physical location, its logical surroundings or relationships, other purposes for which it is being used, or other users. The path the information takes to get to the user may vary, depending on the circumstances under which it is being sought.

From a security standpoint, the point is this: We used to put a great deal of reliance on physical security to protect information. All you needed to do was lock up the computer and restrict access to a few trusted people. As we move further and further along the path to large logical repositories of data that, although logically related to one another, are physically dispersed, physical security takes a back seat to control of the logical access. An example will help make the point.

You are the marketing director of USGUYS, a large multisite, multiproduct company. Ten years ago, the marketing management of each product was pretty much bound to the location where it was produced. Each site produced marketing projections, performance figures, and the like on its products. Then they were sent on to you in corporate HQ for consolidation and analysis. If you wanted more information, you asked for it and hoped for the best. This was the so-called vertical structure.

Today, courtesy of networks and databases, USGUYS has gone horizontal or functional. Instead of individual marketing units within each location, there is a companywide marketing function under single management. To help that along, all USGUYS' marketing data have been consolidated into one set of consistent images or views, even though they still originate and are located at individual sites.

Now, anyone with a need to know (or perhaps without one) anywhere can call up the data they require in order to determine, for example, whether one product has a drag-along effect on another. You can prepare a report or a spreadsheet from a number of related data elements, regardless of where they are physically.

A database is *not*, as is commonly assumed, a physical collection of data. It is a complex directory of data descriptions, data relations, and directions to data. If you can adequately describe the data, today's database management systems can find and assemble the data, even if they are spread over a network of **systems** and communications lines from Raleigh to Rangoon. That puts a whole new dimension on control, authorization, classification, backup, audit trails, and all the other IP issues discussed in this book.

In the future, there will be larger, more diverse, logical data repositories supported by vast numbers of individual physical processors from mainframes to micros, by storage devices ranging from huge direct access storage device (DASD) farms to portable hand-held storage units. Access to all of this will be provided by dynamically switchable public and private networks.

A technologist's dream? No. It's here now. Is the demand there? You bet! Look at your own organization. Consider that, right now, you have no idea where or to whom you are being physically connected when you dial an 800 number. You also have less and less awareness of where or by whom the processing is being done when you present yourself to an automatic teller machine or a point of sale terminal.

Tomorrow there will be more of the same. All of the security and control issues will also be there. You won't know where the data are coming from, who the owners are, or who else is involved in the process. You may not care. But the system must maintain an orderly process, keeping conflicting requirements from getting in each other's way, maintaining data integrity, establishing priorities, and making sure that users get what they are authorized to get—no more, no less.

To counter the control problems associated with this situation, more reliable access control functions, especially replacements for passwords, and more stringent authorization schemes are going to be needed. The technology that will make a major contribution here is the smart card. You've probably seen or even used a smart card, although you may not have recognized it as such. Essentially, the smart card is a plastic card with a microchip or chips embedded in it. (Yes, they can make chips that thin and flexible. I have bent smart cards around thin metal cylinders.) They come in two basic varieties:

1. *The memory card.* This card is simply an expansion of the magnetic stripe card. It contains a lot more information on its microchip than can be put in a magnetic strip. This expanded storage has a lot of uses, such as storing large amounts of identification and verification data to be used in granting access to functions or facilities. The data can be encrypted so that they can be read only by an authorized unit. The memory card requires a special reader that can inquire into the contents of the chip. Typically the chip is read-only.

Unless you have very special equipment, there is no way you can alter it without destroying the contents.

2. *The on-board processor.* The current versions have amazing capabilities, and they are getting more capable. These too have storage, but they are true computers as well. These devices can interact with other processors. Although they also require a reading device, these cards are active. They can participate in a process instead of just waiting for a device to read its contents. Remember the description I gave you in Chapter 9 of challenge-driven tokens to replace the password? Many of them are smart cards with on-board processors.

Information and Process Portability

There are several skills a successful consultant needs that they don't tell you about until you've been in the firm for a while. One is the ability to handle the keyboard and a mouse on a personal computer. The other skill is to be able to behave like a well-trained, high-stamina pack animal. Consultants' information expands to fill all available receptacles, luggage, desk space, floor space, and any other kind of space. We carry tons of stuff with us, including portable PCs, phones, and occasionally fax machines. Portable and car-based phones are becoming common. Jacks in hotels for connecting modems and fax machines are readily available. Not only have data become widely distributed and independent of any single physical source, but the users are on the loose too.

You can no longer trust physical location or device description to tell you who other users are or whether they are authorized. When terminals were "hard wired" into a computer, I had a level of confidence that the device being used on the other end of the line, at least, was known. Also, given a certain amount of physical security, personnel management, an ID and a password, I could establish that the user was known and authorized. Dial-up links from homes or portables on the road (literally) provide none of that physical verification. Further, if you are walking around with a portable computer, the information in that machine may be worth many times what the machine itself is valued at.

Notebook PCs are making portability more realistic. Is the next step to integrate intelligent phones, faxes, and notebook PCs? Could be. But when you lose or misuse one of those, you can really foul things up.

We have the potential for dynamically linked, logically connected, worldwide databases being available to roving users with their own high-powered computing, storage, and communications capabilities. All the necessary technology is here. The demand is beginning to show itself more and more strongly. Security, however, is lagging behind.

Because of these phenomena, I believe that one technology that has been waiting in the wings for a long time may actually get a chance to do a star turn—encryption. Encryption has always had the aura of being super high tech, slightly shady, intelligence community-driven, and, probably most important, expensive and hard to use. Parts of that reputation are well-deserved, but the reputation for being expensive and hard to use is disappearing. Encryption can serve two purposes: protecting transmitted data during transmission and protecting stored data, which can also mean software. Both are important in this scenario for portable-based access to widely distributed data. Encryption can also be a valuable technology in support of message and identity authentication. It's been available to the private sector since the late 1970s, but I believe it will get its turn on stage in the mid-1990s.

Instant Global Communication

It's tough to have true distribution and a roving user base without significant communications capability. Global communications means just that—anywhere you want to connect to. The war in the Persian Gulf gave people a tangible expression of just how global and instantaneous communications can be. For the first time, worldwide civilization witnessed a war almost as it was being fought. Instant worldwide communication is here and, in fact, there is more capacity than there is traffic at this writing.

Volume can be measured several ways: number of individual messages, number of users, or the gross amount of data being transmitted. Currently, a relatively small community of users (banks and other financial services, multinationals, airlines, the military, governments) accounts for most of the intercontinental data message traffic and a substantial part of the voice traffic as well. (Fax is usually regarded as voice traffic because it employs voice telephone technology.) Some technologies, especially television and high resolution images, are great bandwidth hogs. The number of users varies.

Two security questions arise. One is: How do you protect such a complex and colossal infrastructure against failure, compromise, or attack? Currently, the answer is piecemeal, which is not such a bad approach. When you consider the number of different entities—private and public sector—that make up the international communications arena, it's sometimes amazing that anything at all gets communicated. The current trend is toward more organizational fragmentation. The thing that keeps everything on the rails is international standardization, and more security and continuity standards activities are necessary.

The international standards program for encryption, for example, has been a political hassle for years. The banking community and the airlines are probably the two private-sector groups that have gone the farthest in establishing protective standards. A lot more needs to be done if electronic data interchange (EDI), for example, is to work safely in a global arena. There are standards groups in motion, but they could use a lot more support from the private sector. What they are doing is very important with long-lasting effects.

The second question is: By connecting to any network, are you opening yourself up to potential attack from sources you don't even know about? When you open up to a dial-up network, what have you opened up to? Answer: A lot more than you realize.

For reasons that are sometimes a bit difficult to justify, most of us assume that the communications lines we use are safe, that our privacy is not being violated, and that no one out there is trying to do us harm. Perhaps, since so few of us have ever been consciously aware of a telecommunications-related crime, we tend to regard the whole environment as safe. Perhaps, even more typical of human nature, we put the whole process in the back of our minds.

Caution, oddly enough, is not regarded as a particularly attractive virtue. Taking precautions on the phone or phone equivalent is usually regarded as paranoia, but we're reaching the stage where a little paranoia wouldn't hurt.

Multimedia Presentation

The IP issue here is: Now more than ever before, you can't believe everything you see or hear. Time was, a photograph was a pretty conclusive piece of evidence because tampering with a photographic image was difficult, and it usually showed. No more. A signature on a printed document was considered a pretty good piece of evidence too, but not when you have high-resolution color graphics printers and copiers. And can you always tell whether the voice on the other end of a phone is real or computer-generated?

This is another area where the technology to *do* has outstripped the technology to *control*. There are legal, social, and technological issues here that need a lot of attention and exercise. There are a number of potential applications here for the electronic envelope, signature, and other authentication techniques I outlined in Chapter 9.

The Paperless Transaction

This is one the auditors love. How do you trace a paper trail when there are no documents to trace? There are a lot of paperless transactions in use today. Many of us get our pay deposited directly through electronic funds transfer. You may pay your bills the same way. EDI is designed to do away with the purchase order, invoice, and perhaps even the contract as we know it.

Can you make an electronic bit stream fit the same rules for proof of transaction that you used with a paper document, especially if no document exists *in any form,* electronic or otherwise? There are probably just a couple of table entries indicating that a transaction was triggered. The transaction itself is probably no more than a few digits of code. The result could be the movement of millions of dollars in goods. Can the authorization, time of transaction, receipt, and action taken all be traced with the same accuracy as or greater accuracy than the paper system?

The answer is yes. However, it requires a great deal more attention to control and protection in the design and development process than seems to be happening today. Trying to retrofit controls on these kinds of processes is expensive, clumsy, inefficient, and often impossible. They need to be developed within the system. The control and security specialists need a new set of skills—design and development skills. There are a fair number of folks who can accurately assess and even make recommendations on how to improve security and continuity. There are far too few who know how to make it happen. We are trying to improve that breed. You can help by acknowledging the need, encouraging the growth of such individuals, and providing the wherewithal to make it happen.

The Future

The fact of the matter is that one of the major attractions of the future is its unknowability. In the whole arena of information technology, change has happened more rapidly and with greater impact than most of us have been able to predict. Nor has the obvious always been the way things turned out. Some sure-fire technologies dove into oblivion. Some great applications were resisted by the target buyers. Some burning issues turned out to be duds. Others, like the virus, came out of left field. The fact is we don't know much about the future except that it tends to come faster and more strongly than we assume. It wouldn't hurt to have a little protection around to deal with it.

Throughout this book, I've tried not to alarm or discourage. The exposures and threats to information resources are real, and I've tried to present them realistically, but also real are the opportunities, technologies, and methods to deal with these exposures and threats.

The real opportunity is to *improve* your systems, applications, and information, and thus improve your enterprise.

Glossary

application A task to be performed by a computer program(s) or system(s). Simply put, applications run on systems.

continuity Preventing, mitigating, and recovering from disruption. The terms *business resumption planning, disaster recovery planning,* and *contingency planning* may also be used in this context; they concentrate on the recovery aspects of continuity.

continuity assessment See **security assessment.**

control Covers such things as data entry, design, procedure, and accounting errors.

data See **information.**

EDP Electronic data processing. (The U.S. government uses the term *ADP* for automatic data processing.)

EDP audit Often referred to as computer audit. The EDP auditor's primary responsibility is to inform the nontechnical financial auditor (internal or external) about the state of control in computer-based financial systems, but may also deal with nonfinancial systems and many subjects associated with information protection.

information Data to which some judgment has been added. (The issue of data versus information is not important for our purposes.)

information protection (IP) The prevention of, and recovery from, unauthorized disruption, modification, disclosure, or use of information and information resources, whether accidental or deliberate. Or, if you prefer a more positive statement: the preservation of the integrity, confidentiality, and availability of information and information resources.

information resources The information itself, computers, and other processing hardware, software, telecommunications, and the related support infrastructure such as power, light, and air conditioning; but the most important information resource is people.

platform Usually refers to a specific hardware or software system technology, for example, a Digital Equipment VAX-VMS platform or an IBM AS/400 platform. In the area of personal computers, the major platforms are IBM-compatible and MAC-compatible.

privacy A legal and social concept related to information protection. The major point of connection is in preserving confidentiality.

recovery The state when information processing functions are operational again following a disruption.

resources See **information resources.**

restoration The state when everything is back to normal following a disruption, including cleaning up the backlog of transactions that may have been processed in an alternative mode.

risk acceptance A process based on a combination of risk assessments and security and/or continuity assessments by which management decides what level of business risk is prudent to accept.

risk assessment A method for determining the probability (and sometimes the potential impact) of security- or continuity-related threats. Usually results in a prioritized list of risks. Related to asset valuation (what are the assets worth?) and vulnerability assessment (if the threat occurs, how likely are we to be damaged by it?).

risk management Related to, but different from, information protection. Deals with areas such as criminal and terrorist activities, safety, protection of key executives, and insurance programs.

security Maintaining the integrity of and controlling access to information and resources.

security assessment A method for determining the effectiveness of security or continuity measures in dealing with security- or continuity-related risks. There is an obvious connection between this and risk assessment, and they are often lumped together. In this book, I keep them separate.

system A composite of equipment, skills, techniques, and information capable of performing and/or supporting an operational role in attaining specified management objectives.

Bibliography

I have listed here a small number of books and periodicals that I believe may be of further assistance to the business manager in developing an information protection program. This bibliography is by no means a complete record of all the works and sources available on the subject and its related issues. I have omitted texts which are primarily technical in nature or narrowly specialized in one area. Several of the authors listed below have written a number of works on or related to information protection. Not all of their works may be mentioned here. The omission of an author or one or several books or articles from this list does not mean that I have made any sort of value judgement regarding that author and/or that work.

Abrams, M.D. and H.J. Podell, *Computer and Network Security.* Los Alamitos, Calif.: IEEE Computer Society, 1987.

AFIPS Federal and State Legislative Update. American Federation of Information Processing Societies, Inc. (A reference source for legislation that might effect you). Updated periodically.

Baskerville, Richard. *Designing Information Systems Security.* New York: John Wiley & Sons, Inc., 1988.

BloomBecker, Jay (ed.). Introduction to Computer Crime, Los Angeles: National Center for Computer Crime Data, 1985.

Carroll, John M. *Computer Security*, 2nd edition. Stoneham, Mass.: Butterworth Publishers, 1987.

Computer Security Products Report. Assets Protection. (An annual buyer's guide to equipment and services and a vendor directory.)

Data Security Management. Auerbach Publishers, 1982. (A comprehensive reference service.) Updated bimonthly.

Datapro Reports on Information Security. Datapro Research Corp. (A comprehensive information service.) Updated monthly.

Denning, Peter (ed.). *Computers Under Attack: Intruders, Worms and Viruses.* New York: ACM Press, 1990.

FitzGerald, Jerry. *Business Data Communications: Basic Concepts, Security and Design.* New York: John Wiley & Sons, 1984.

————. *Designing Controls Into Computerized Systems.* Redwood City, Calif.: Jerry FitzGerald and Associates, 1981.

Institute of Internal Auditors. *Systems Auditability and Control Reports.* New York: Institute of Internal Auditors, 1991.

Krull, Alan R. *Ownership and Accountability: A Framework for DP Asset Protection.* White Plains, N.Y.: IBM Information Systems Management Institute, 1984.

Lobel, Jerome. *Foiling the Security Breakers: Computer Security and Access Control.* New York: McGraw-Hill Book Company, 1986.

O'Donoghue, Joseph. *The 1986 Mercy College Report on Computer Crime in the Forbes 500 Corporations: The Strategies of Containment.* Dobbs Ferry, N.Y.: Mercy College, 1986.

Office of Technology Assessment, U.S. Congress. *Intellectual Property Rights in an Age of Electronics and Information* (OTA-CIT-302). Washington, D.C., 1986.

Parker, Donn B. *Computer Security Management.* Englewood Cliffs, N.J.: Prentice Hall, 1981.

————. *The Malicious Computer Hacker Problem.* SRI International, 1984.

Schweitzer, James A. *Computer Crime and Business Information: A Practical Guide for Managers.* New York: Elsevier Science Publishing Co., Inc. 1986.

————. *Protecting Information in the Electronic Workplace.* Englewood Cliffs, N.J.: Prentice Hall, 1983.

Steinauer, Dennis D. *Security of Personal Computer Systems: A Management Guide* (NBS SP500-120). Washington, D.C.: Department of Commerce, National Institute of Standards and Technology, 1985.

Stoll, Clifford, *The Cuckoo's Egg,* New York: Doubleday & Co., Inc., 1989.

The following magazines specialize in information protection subjects:

Crisis Magazine, Robert Bogle, publisher, Wayne, Penn.

Contingency Journal, Bob Thomas, publisher, Dallas, Texas.

Disaster Recovery Journal, Richard Arnold, publisher, St. Louis, Missouri.

ISPNews: Info Security Product News, Michael Sobol, publisher, Framingham, Mass.

Index

227